A Study of Shakespeare

Swinburne, Algernon Charles

Contents

LA GRANDE BRETECHE 7

A STUDY OF SHAKESPEARE

BY

Swinburne, Algernon Charles

TO JAMES ORCHARD HALLIWELL-PHILLIPPS.

That a sample or excerpt given from this book while as yet save in design unfinished should have found such favour in your sight and won such approval at your hands as you then by word alike and action so cordially expressed, is reason enough why I should inscribe it with your name: even if I felt less pleasure in the reflection and the record that this little labour of a lifelong love had at once the doubly good fortune and the doubly grateful success, to be praised by those who have earned the praise and thanks of all true Shakespearean scholars, and dispraised by such as have deserved their natural doom to reap neither but from the harvest of their own applause or that of their fellows. It might be hard for a personally unbiassed judgment to strike the balance of genuine value and significance between these two forms of acknowledgment: but it will be evident which is to me the more precious, when I write your name above my own on the votive scroll which attaches my offering to the shrine of Shakespeare.

ALGERNON CHARLES SWINBURNE.

A STUDY OF SHAKESPEARE.

I

THE greatest poet of our age has drawn a parallel of elaborate eloquence between Shakespeare and the sea; and the likeness holds good in many points of less significance than those which have been set down by the master-hand. For two hundred years at least have students of every kind put forth in every sort of boat on a longer or a shorter voyage of research across the waters of that unsounded sea. From the paltriest fishing-craft to such majestic galleys as were steered by Coleridge and by Goethe, each division of the fleet has done or has essayed its turn of work; some busied in dredging alongshore, some taking surveys of this or that gulf or headland, some putting forth through shine and shadow into the darkness of the great deep. Nor does it seem as if there would sooner be an end to men's labour on this than on the other sea. But here a difference is perceptible. The material ocean has been so far mastered by the wisdom and the heroism of man that we may look for a time to come when the mystery shall be manifest of its furthest north and south, and men resolve the secret of the uttermost parts of the sea: the poles also may find their Columbus. But the limits of that other ocean, the laws of its tides, the motive of its forces, the mystery of its unity and the secret of its change, no seafarer of us all may ever think thoroughly to know. No wind-gauge will help us to the science of its storms, no lead-line sound for us the depth of its divine and terrible serenity.

As, however, each generation for some two centuries now or more has witnessed fresh attempts at pilotage and fresh expeditions of discovery undertaken in the seas of Shakespeare, it may be well to study a little the laws of navigation in such waters as these, and look well to compass and rudder before we accept the guidance of a strange helmsman or make proffer for trial of our own. There are shoals and quicksands on which many a seafarer has run his craft aground in time past, and others of more special peril to adventurers of the present day. The chances of shipwreck vary in a certain degree with each new change of vessel and each fresh muster of hands. At one time a main rock of offence on which the stoutest ships of discovery were wont to split was the narrow and slippery reef of verbal emendation; and upon this our native pilots were too many of them prone to steer. Others fell becalmed offshore in a German fog of philosophic theories, and would not be persuaded that the house of words they had built in honour of Shakespeare was "dark as hell," seeing "it had bay-windows transparent as barricadoes, and the clear-stories towards the south-north were as lustrous as; ebony." These are not the most besetting dangers of more modern steersmen: what we have to guard against now is neither a repetition of the pedantries of Steevens nor a recrudescence of the moralities of; Ulrici. Fresh follies spring up in new paths of criticism, and fresh labourers in a fruitless field are: at hand to gather them and to garner. A discovery of some importance has recently been proclaimed as with blare of vociferous trumpets and flutter of triumphal flags; no less a discovery than this—that a singer must be tested by his song. Well, it is something that criticism should at length be awake to that wholly indisputable fact; that learned and laborious men who can hear only with their I fingers should open their eyes to admit such a novelty, their minds to accept such a paradox, as that a painter should be studied in his pictures and a poet in his verse. To the common herd of students and lovers of either art this may perhaps appear no great discovery; but that it should at length have dawned even upon the race of commentators is a sign which in itself might be taken as a presage of new light to come in an epoch of miracle yet to be, Unhappily it is as yet but a partial revelation that has been vouchsafed to them. To the recognition of the apocalyptic fact that a workman can only be known by his work, and that without examination of his method and material that work can hardly be studied to much purpose, they have yet to add the knowledge of a further truth no less recondite and abstruse than this; that as the technical work of a painter appeals to the eye, so the technical work of a poet appeals to the ear. It follows that men who have none are as likely to arrive at any profitable end by the application of metrical tests to the work of Shakespeare as a blind man by the application of his theory of colours to the work of Titian.

It is certainly no news to other than professional critics that no means of study can be more precious or more necessary to a student of Shakespeare than this of tracing the course of his work by the growth and development, through various modes and changes, of his metre. But the faculty of using such means of study is not to be had for the asking; it is not to be earned by the most assiduous toil, it is not to be secured by the learning of years, it is not to be attained by the devotion of a life. No proficiency in grammar and arithmetic, no science of numeration and no scheme of prosody, will be here of the least avail. Though the pedagogue were Briareus himself who would thus bring Shakespeare under the rule of his rod or Shelley within the limit of his line, he would lack fingers on which to count the syllables that make up their music, the infinite varieties of measure that complete the changes and the chimes of perfect verse. It is but lost labour that they rise up so early, and so late take rest; not a Scaliger or Salmasius of them all will sooner solve the riddle of the simplest than of the subtlest melody, Least of all will the method of a scholiast be likely to serve him as a clue to the hidden things of Shakespeare. For all the counting up of numbers and casting up of figures that a whole university—nay, a whole universe of pedants could accomplish, no teacher and no learner will ever be a whit the nearer to the haven where they would be. In spite of all tabulated statements and regulated summaries of research, the music which will not be dissected or defined, the "spirit of sense" which is one and indivisible from the body or the raiment of speech that clothes it, keeps safe the secret of its sound. Yet it is no less a task than this that the scholiasts have girt themselves to achieve: they will pluck out the heart not of Hamlet's but of Shakespeare's mystery by the means of a metrical test; and this test is to be applied by a purely arithmetical process. It is useless to pretend or to protest that they work by any rule but the rule of thumb and finger: that they have no ear to work by, whatever outward show they may make of unmistakable ears, the very nature of their project gives full and damning proof. Properly understood, this that they call the metrical test is doubtless, as they say, the surest or the sole sure key to one side of the secret of Shakespeare; but they will never understand it properly who propose to secure it by the ingenious device of numbering the syllables and tabulating the results of a computation which shall attest in exact sequence the quantity, order, and proportion of single and double endings, of rhyme and blank verse, of regular lines and irregular, to be traced in each play by the horny eye and the callous finger of a pedant. "I am ill at these numbers"; those in which I have sought to become an expert are numbers of another sort; but having, from wellnigh the first years I can remember, made of the study of Shakespeare the chief intellectual business and found in it the chief spiritual delight of my whole life, I can hardly think myself less qualified than another to offer an opinion on the metrical points at issue.

The progress and expansion of style and harmony in the successive works of Shakespeare must in some indefinite degree be perceptible to the youngest as to the oldest, to the dullest as to the keenest of Shakespearean students. But to trace and verify the various shades and gradations of this progress, the ebb and flow of alternate influences, the delicate and infinite subtleties of change and growth discernible in the spirit and the speech of the greatest among poets, is a task not less beyond the reach of a scholiast than beyond the faculties of a child. He who would attempt it with any chance of profit must above all things remember at starting that the inner and the outer qualities of a poet's work are of their very nature indivisible; that any criticism is of necessity worthless which looks to one side only, whether it be to the outer or to the inner quality of the work; that the fatuity of pedantic ignorance never devised a grosser absurdity than the attempt to separate æsthetic from scientific criticism by a strict line of demarcation, and to bring all critical work under one or the other head of this exhaustive division. Criticism without accurate science of the thing criticised can indeed have no other value than may belong to the genuine record of a spontaneous impression; but it is not less certain that criticism which busies itself only with the outer husk or technical shell of a great artist's work, taking no account of the spirit or the thought which informs it, cannot have even so much value as this. Without study of his forms of metre or his scheme of colours we shall certainly fail to appreciate or even to apprehend the gist or the worth of a painter's or a poet's design; but to note down the number of special words and cast up the sum of superfluous syllables used once or twice or twenty times in the Structure of a single poem will help us exactly as much as a naked catalogue of the colours employed in a particular picture. A tabulated statement or summary of the precise number of blue or green, red or white draperies to be found in a precise number of paintings by the same hand will not of itself afford much enlightenment to any but the youngest of possible students; nor will a mere list of double or single, masculine or feminine terminations discoverable in a given amount of verse from the same quarter prove of much use on benefit to an adult reader of common intelligence. What such an one requires is the guidance which can be given by no metremonger or colour-grinder: the suggestion which may help him to discern at once the cause and the effect of every choice or change of metre and of colour; which may show him at one glance the reason and the result of every shade and of every tone which tends to compose and to complete the gradual scale of their final harmonies. This method of study is generally accepted as the only one applicable to the work of a great painter by any criticism worthy of the name: it should also be recognised as the sole method by which the work of a great poet can be studied to any serious purpose. For the student it can be no less useful, for the expert it should be no less easy, to trace through its several stages of expansion and transfiguration the genius of Chaucer or of Shakespeare, of Milton or of Shelley, than the genius of Titian or of Raffaelle, of Turner or of Rossetti. Some great artists there are of either kind in whom no such process of growth or transformation is perceptible: of these are Coleridge and Blake; from the sunrise to the sunset of their working day we can trace no demonstrable increase and no visible diminution of the divine capacities or the inborn defects of either man's genius; but not of such, as a rule, are the greatest among artists of any sort.

Another rock on which modern steersmen of a more skilful hand than these are yet liable to run through too much confidence is the love of their own conjectures as to the actual date or the secret history of a particular play or passage. To err on this side requires more thought, more learning, and more ingenuity than we need think to find in a whole tribe of finger-counters and figure-casters; but the outcome of these good gifts, if strained or perverted to capricious use, may prove no less barren of profit than the labours of a pedant on the letter of the text. It is a tempting exercise of intelligence for a dexterous and keen-witted scholar to apply his solid learning and his vivid fancy to the detection or the interpretation of some new or obscure point in a great man's life or work; but none the less is it a perilous pastime to give the reins to a learned fancy, and let loose conjecture on the trail of any dubious crotchet or the scent of any supposed allusion that may spring up in the way of its confident and eager quest. To start a new solution of some crucial problem, to track some new undercurrent of concealed significance in a passage hitherto neglected or misconstrued, is to a critic of this higher class a delight as keen as that of scientific discovery to students of another sort: the pity is that he can bring no such certain or immediate test to verify the value of his discovery as lies ready to the hand of the man of science. Whether he have lit upon a windfall or a mare's nest can be decided by no direct proof, but only by time and the general acceptance of competent judges; and this cannot often be reasonably expected for theories which can appeal for support or confirmation to no positive evidence, but at best to a cloudy and shifting probability. What personal or political allusions may lurk under the text of Shakespeare we can never know, and should consequently forbear to hang upon a hypothesis of this floating and nebulous kind any serious opinion which might gravely affect our estimate of his work or his position in regard to other men, with whom some public or private interest may possibly have brought him into contact or collision. When, however, such a wealth and weight of learning, such brilliancy and fertility of conjecture, have together been brought to bear upon this question as we have seen of late years applied to it, we cannot but hope that some real light may be struck out on the subject in passing; and even if we get none sure or strong enough to steer by in safety towards any actual port of belief, we may thankfully enjoy the new knowledge and the fresh illustration supplied by such labours as those of the editor of the **Siege of Antwerp,** the first and (to the keen disappointment I should think of many students besides myself) the last instalment issued during the editor's lifetime of a series projected under the title of **The School of Shakespeare,** or the author of some articles in the last numbers published of the **North British Review,** on the supposed secret meanings and latent controversies traceable in the works of Shakespeare, Jonson, and their several satellites or subordinates, antagonists or allies. Absolute confidence or positive belief we need not feel bound or inclined to accord to the conjectures of such writers; but from the treasures of their critical and historical scholarship, from the acute and strenuous exercise of the energies of their thought, from the ardour of study and intelligence devoted to matters of such keen interest to us all, it must be our own fault and our own loss if we fail to carry away any sense of profit or impression of enjoyment. And this we may do while guarding ourselves against the temptation to assume or to accept as matter of established fact any theory, though never so ingenious, which has no evident footing on the solid ground of proof.

The aim of the present study is simply to set down what the writer believes to be certain demonstrable truths as to the progress and development of style, the outer and the inner changes of manner as of matter, of method as of design, which may be discerned in the work of Shakespeare. The principle here adopted and the views here put forward have not been suddenly discovered or lightly taken up out of any desire to make a show of theoretical ingenuity. For years past I have held and maintained, in private discussion with friends and fellow-students, the opinions which I now submit to more public judgment. How far they may coincide with those advanced by others I cannot say, and have not been careful to inquire. The mere fact of coincidence or of dissent on such a question is of less importance than the principle accepted by either student as the groundwork of his theory, the mainstay of his opinion. It is no part of my project or my hope to establish the actual date of any among the various plays, or to determine point by point the lineal order of their succession. I have examined no table or catalogue of recent or of earlier date, from the time of Malone onwards, with a view to confute by my reasoning the conclusions of another, or by the assistance of his theories to corroborate my own. It is impossible to fix or decide by inner or outer evidence the precise order of production, much less of composition, which critics of the present or the past may have set their wits to verify in vain; but it is quite possible to show that the work of Shakespeare is naturally divisible into classes which may serve us to distinguish and determine as by landmarks the several stages or periods of his mind and art.

Of these the three chief periods or stages are so unmistakably indicated by the mere text itself, and so easily recognisable by the veriest tiro in the school of Shakespeare, that even were I as certain of being the first to point them out as I am conscious of having long since discovered and verified them without assistance or suggestion from any but Shakespeare himself, I should be disposed to claim but little credit for a discovery which must in all likelihood have been forestalled by the common insight of some hundred or more students in time past The difficulty begins with the really debatable question of subdivisions. There are certain plays which maybe said to hang on the borderland between one period and the next, with one foot lingering and one advanced; and these must be classed according to the dominant note of their style, the greater or lesser proportion of qualities proper to the earlier or the later stage of thought and writing. At one time I was inclined to think the whole catalogue more accurately divisible into four classes; but the line of demarcation between the third and fourth would have been so much fainter than those which mark off the first period from the second, and the second from the third, that it seemed on the whole a more correct and adequate arrangement to assume that the last period might be subdivided if necessary into a first and second stage. This somewhat precise and pedantic scheme of study I have adopted from no love of rigid or formal system, but simply to make the method of my critical process as clear as the design. That design is to examine by internal evidence alone the growth and the expression of spirit and of speech, the ebb and flow of thought and style, discernible in the successive periods of Shakespeare's work; to study the phases of mind, the changes of tone, the passage or progress from an old manner to a new, the reversion or relapse from a later to an earlier habit, which may assuredly be traced in the modulations of his varying verse, but can only be traced by ear and not by finger, I have busied myself with no baseless speculations as to the possible or probable date of the first appearance of this play or of that on the stage; and it is not unlikely that the order of succession here adopted or suggested may not always coincide with the chronological order of production; nor will the principle or theory by which I have undertaken to class the successive plays of each period be affected or impaired though it should chance that a play ranked by me as belonging to a later stage of work should actually have been produced earlier than others which in my lists are assigned to a subsequent date. It is not, so to speak, the literal but the spiritual order which I have studied to observe and to indicate: the periods which I seek to define belong not to chronology but to art. No student need be reminded how common a thing it is to recognise in the later work of a great artist some partial reappearance of his early tone or manner, some passing return to his early lines of work and to habits of style since modified or abandoned. Such work, in part at least,, may properly be said to belong rather to the earlier stage whose manner it resumes than to the later stage at which it was actually produced, and in which it stands out as a marked exception among the works of the same period. A famous and a most singularly beautiful example of this reflorescence as in a Saint Martin's summer of undecaying genius is the exquisite and crowning love-scene in the opera or "ballet-tragedy" of *Psyche,* written in his sixty-fifth year by the august Roman hand of Pierre Corneille; a lyric symphony of spirit and of song fulfilled with all the colour and all the music that autumn could steal from spring if October had leave to go a Maying in some Olympian masque rade of melody and sunlight. And it is not easier easy as it is, to discern and to define the three main stages of Shakespeare's work and progress, than to classify under their several heads the representative plays belonging to each period by the law of their nature, if not by the accident of their date. There are certain dominant qualities which do on the whole distinguish not only the later from the earlier plays, but the second period from the first the third period from the second; and it is with these qualities alone that the higher criticism, be it æsthetic or scientific, has properly anything to do.

A new method of solution has been applied to various difficulties which have been discovered or invented in the text by the care or the perversity of recent commentators, whose principle of explanation is easier to abuse than to use with any likelihood of profit. It is at least simple enough for the simplest of critics to apply or misapply: whenever they see or suspect an inequality or an incongruity which may be wholly imperceptible to eyes uninured to the use of their spectacles, they assume at once the presence of another workman, the intrusion of a stranger's hand. This supposition of a double authorship is naturally as impossible to refute as to establish by other than internal evidence and appeal to the private judgment or perception of the reader. But it is no better than the last resource of an empiric, the last refuge of a sciolist; a refuge which the soundest of scholars will be slowest to seek, a resource which the most competent of critics will be least ready to adopt. Once admitted as a principle of general application, there are no lengths to which it may not carry, there are none to which it has not carried, the audacious fatuity and the arrogant incompetence of tamperers with the authentic text. Recent editors who have taken on themselves the high office of guiding English youth in its first study of Shakespeare have proposed to excise or to obelise whole passages which the delight and wonder of youth and age alike, of the rawest as of the ripest among students, have agreed to consecrate as examples of his genius at its highest. In the last trumpet-notes of Macbeth's defiance and despair, in the last rallying cry of the hero reawakened in the tyrant at his utmost hour of need, there have been men and scholars, Englishmen and editors, who have detected the alien voice of a pretender, the false ring of a foreign blast that was not blown by Shakespeare; words that for centuries past have touched with fire the hearts of thousands in each age since they were first inspired—words with the whole sound in them of battle or a breaking sea, with the whole soul of pity and terror mingled and melted into each other in the fierce last speech of a spirit grown "aweary of the sun," have been calmly transferred from the account of Shakespeare to the score of Middleton. And this, forsooth, the student of the future is to accept on the authority of men who bring to the support of their decision the unanswerable plea of years spent in the collation and examination of texts never hitherto explored and compared with such energy of learned labour. If this be the issue of learning and of industry, the most indolent and ignorant of readers who retains his natural capacity to be moved and mastered by the natural delight of contact with heavenly things is better off by far than the most studious and strenuous of all scholiasts who ever claimed acquiescence or challenged dissent on the strength of his lifelong labours and hard-earned knowledge of the letter of the text. Such an one is indeed "in a parlous state"; and any boy whose heart first begins to burn within him, who feels his blood kindle and his spirit dilate, his pulse leap and his eyes lighten, over a first study of Shakespeare, may say to such a teacher with better reason than Touchstone said to Corin, "Truly, thou art damned; like an ill-roasted egg, all on one side." Nor could charity itself hope much profit for him from the moving appeal and the pious prayer which temper that severity of sentence—"Wilt thou rest damned? God help thee, shallow man! God make incision in thee! Thou art raw." And raw he is like to remain for all his learning, and for all incisions that can be made in the horny hide of a self-conceit to be pierced by the puncture of no man's pen. It was bad enough while theorists of this breed confined themselves to the suggestion of a possible partnership with Fletcher, a possible interpolation by Jonson; but in the descent from these to the alleged adulteration of the text by Middleton and Rowley we have surely sounded the very lowest depth of folly attainable by the utmost alacrity in sinking which may yet be possible to the bastard brood of Scriblerus. For my part, I shall not be surprised though the next discoverer should assure us that half at least of **Hamlet** is evidently due to the collaboration of Heywood, while the greater part of **Othello** is as clearly assignable to the hand of Shirley.

Akin to this form of folly, but less pernicious though not more profitable, is the fancy of inventing some share for Shakespeare in the composition of plays which the veriest insanity of conjecture or caprice could not venture to lay wholly to his charge. This fancy, comparatively harmless as it is, requires no ground of proof to go upon, no prop of likelihood to support it; without so much help as may be borrowed from the faintest and most fitful of traditions, it spins its own evidence spider like out of its own inner conscience or conceit, and proffers it with confident complacency for men' acceptance. Here again I cannot but see a mere waste of fruitless learning and bootless ingenuity. That Shakespeare began by retouching and recasting the work of elder and lesser men we all know; that he may afterwards have set his hand to the task of adding or altering a line or a passage here and there in some few of the plays brought out under his direction as manager or proprietor of a theatre is of course possible, but can neither be affirmed nor denied with any profit in default of the least fragment of historic or traditional evidence. Any attempt to verify the imaginary touch of his hand in plays of whose history we know no more than that they were acted on the boards of his theatre can be but a diversion for the restless leisure of ingenious and ambitious scholars; it will give no clue by which the student who simply seeks to know what can be known with certainty of the poet and his work may hope to be guided towards any safe issue or trustworthy result. Less pardonable and more presumptuous than this is the pretension of minor critics to dissect an authentic play of Shakespeare scene by scene, and assign different parts of the same poem to different dates by the same pedagogic rules of numeration and mensuration which they would apply to the general question of the order and succession of his collective works. This vivisection of a single poem is not defensible as a freak of scholarship, an excursion beyond the bounds of bare proof, from which the wanderer may chance to bring back, if not such treasure as he went out to seek, yet some stray godsend or rare literary windfall which may serve to excuse his indulgence in the seemingly profitless pastime of a truant disposition. It is a pure impertinence to affirm with oracular assurance what might perhaps be admissible as a suggestion offered with the due diffidence of modest and genuine scholarship; to assert on the strength of a private pedant's personal intuition that such must be the history or such the composition of a great work whose history he alone could tell, whose composition he alone could explain, who gave it to us as his genius had given it to him.

From these several rocks and quicksands I trust at least to keep my humbler course at a safe distance, and steer clear of all sandy shallows of theory or sunken shoals of hypothesis on which no pilot can be certain of safe anchorage; avoiding all assumption, though never so plausible, for which no ground but that of fancy can be shown, all suggestion though never so ingenious for which no proof but that of conjecture can be advanced. For instance, I shall neither assume nor accept the theory of a double authorship or of a double date by which the supposed inequalities may be accounted for, the supposed difficulties may be swept away, which for certain readers disturb the study of certain plays of Shakespeare. Only where universal tradition and the general concurrence of all reasonable critics past and present combine to indicate an unmistakable difference of touch or an unmistakable diversity of date between this and that portion of the same play, or where the internal evidence of interpolation perceptible to the most careless and undeniable by the most perverse of readers is supported by the public judgment of men qualified to express and competent to defend an opinion, have I thought it allowable to adopt this facile method of explanation. No scholar, for example, believes in the single authorship of **Pericles** or **Andronicus;** none, I suppose, would now question the part taken by some hireling or journeyman in the arrangement or completion for the stage of **Timon of Athens;** and few probably would refuse to admit a doubt of the total authenticity or uniform workmanship of the **Taming of the Shrew.** As few, I hope, are prepared to follow the fantastic and confident suggestions of every unquiet and arrogant innovator who may seek to append his name to the long scroll of Shakespearean parasites by the display of a brand-new hypothesis as to the uncertain date or authorship of some passage or some play which has never before been subjected to the scientific scrutiny of such a pertinacious analyst. The more modest design of the present study has in part been already indicated, and will explain as it proceeds if there be anything in it worth explanation. It is no part of my ambition to loose the Gordian knots which others who found them indissoluble have sought in vain to cut in sunder with blunter swords than the Macedonian; but after so many adventures and attempts there may perhaps yet be room for an attempt yet unessayed; for a study by the ear alone of Shakespeare's metrical progress, and a study by light of the knowledge thus obtained of the corresponsive progress within, which found expression and embodiment in these outward and visible changes. The one study will be then seen to be the natural complement and the inevitable consequence of the other; and the patient pursuit of the simpler and more apprehensible object of research will appear as the only sure method by which a reasonable and faithful student may think to attain so much as the porch or entrance to that higher knowledge which no faithful and reasonable study of Shakespeare can ever for a moment fail to keep in sight as the haven of its final hope, the goal of its ultimate labour.

When Christopher Marlowe came up to London from Cambridge, a boy in years, a man in genius, and a god in ambition, he found the stage which he was born to transfigure and re-create by the might and masterdom of his genius encumbered with a litter of rude rhyming farces and tragedies which the first wave of his imperial hand swept so utterly out of sight and hearing that hardly by piecing together such fragments of that buried rubbish as it is now possible to unearth can we rebuild in imagination so much of the rough and crumbling walls that fell before the trumpet-blast of *Tamburlaine* as may give us some conception of the rabble dynasty of rhymers whom he overthrew—of the citadel of dramatic barbarism which was stormed and sacked at the first charge of the young conqueror who came to lead English audiences and to deliver English poetry

> From jigging veins of rhyming mother-wits,
> And such conceit as clownage keeps in pay.

When we speak of the drama that existed before the coming of Marlowe, and that vanished at his advent, we think usually of the rhyming plays written wholly or mainly in ballad verse of fourteen syllables—of the **Kings Darius** and **Camby-**

ses, the ***Promos and Cassandra*** of Whetstone, or the ***Sir Clyomon and Sir Clamydes*** of George Peele. If we turn from these abortions of tragedy to the metrical farces which may fairy be said to contain the germ or embryo of English comedy (a form of dramatic art which certainly owes nothing to the father of our tragic stage), we find far more of hope and promise in the broad free sketches of the flagellant head-master of Eton and the bibulous Bishop of Bath and Wells; and must admit that hands used to wield the crosier or the birch proved themselves more skilful at the lighter labours of the stage, more successful even in the secular and bloodless business of a field neither clerical nor scholastic, than any tragic rival of the opposite party to that so jovially headed by Orbilius Udall and Silenus Still. These twin pillars of church and school and stage were strong enough to support on the shoulders of their authority the first crude fabric or formless model of our comic theatre, while the tragic boards were still creaking and cracking under the jingling canter of ***Cambyses*** or the tuneless tramp of ***Gorboduc.*** This one play which the charity of Sidney excepts from his general anathema on the nascent stage of England has hitherto been erroneously described as written in blank verse; an error which I can only attribute to the prevalence of a groundless assumption that whatever is neither prose nor rhyme must of necessity be definable as blank verse. But the measure, I must repeat, which was adopted by the authors of ***Gorboduc*** is by no means so definable. Blank it certainly is; but verse it assuredly is not. There can be no verse where there is no modulation, no rhythm where there is no music. Blank verse came into life in England at the birth of the shoemaker's son who had but to open his yet beardless lips, and the high-born poem which had Sackville to father and Sidney to sponsor was silenced and eclipsed for ever among the poor plebeian crowd of rhyming shadows that waited in death on the noble nothingness of its patrician shade.

These, I suppose, are the first or the only plays whose names recur to the memory of the general reader when he thinks of the English stage before Marlowe; but there was, I suspect, a whole class of plays then current, and more or less supported by popular favour, of which hardly a sample is now extant, and which cannot be classed with such as these. The poets or rhymesters who supplied them had already seen good to clip the cumbrous and bedraggled skirts of those dreary verses, run all to seed and weed, which jingled their thin bells at the tedious end of fourteen weary syllables; and for this curtailment of the shambling and sprawling lines which had hitherto done duty as tragic metre some credit may be due to these obscure purveyors of forgotten ware for the second epoch of our stage: if indeed, as I presume, we may suppose that this reform, such as it was, had begun before the time of Marlowe; otherwise, no doubt, little credit would be due to men who with so high an example before them were content simply to snip away the tags and fringes, to patch the seams and tatters, of the ragged coat of rhyme which they might have exchanged for that royal robe of heroic verse wherewith he had clothed the ungrown limbs of limping and lisping tragedy. But if these also may be reckoned among his precursors, the dismissal from stage service of the dolorous and drudging metre employed by the earliest school of theatrical rhymesters must be taken to mark a real step in advance; and in that case we possess at least a single example of the rhyming tragedies which had their hour between the last plays written wholly or partially in ballad metre and the first plays written in blank verse. The tragedy of *Selimus, Emperor of the Turks,* published in 1594, may then serve to indicate this brief and obscure period of transition. Whole scenes of this singular play are written in rhyming iambics, some in the measure of *Don Juan,* some in the measure of *Venus and Adonis.* The couplets and quatrains so much affected and so reluctantly abandoned by Shakespeare after the first stage of his dramatic progress are in no other play that I know of diversified by this alternate variation of *sesta* with *ottava rima.* This may have been an exceptional experiment due merely to the caprice of one eccentric rhymester; but in any case we may assume it to mark the extreme limit, the ultimate development of rhyming tragedy after the ballad metre had been happily exploded. The play is on other grounds worth attention as a sign of the times, though on poetical grounds it is assuredly worth none. Part of it is written in blank verse, or at least in rhymeless lines; so that after all it probably followed in the wake of *Tamburlaine,* half adopting and half rejecting the innovations of that fiery reformer, who wrought on the old English stage no less a miracle than *Hernani* on the French stage in the days of our fathers. That *Selimus* was published four years later than *Tamburlaine,* in the year following the death of Marlowe, proves of course nothing as to the date of its production; and even if it was written and acted in the year of its publication, it undoubtedly in the main represents the work of a prior era to the reformation of the stage by Marlowe. The level regularity of its unrhymed scenes is just like that of the weaker portions of *Titus Andronicus* and the *First Part of King Henry the Sixth*—the opening scene, for example, of either play. With *Andronicus* it has also in common the quality of exceptional monstrosity, a delight in the parade of mutilation as well as of massacre. It seems to me possible that the same hand may have been at work on all three plays; for that Marlowe's is traceable in those parts of the two retouched by Shakespeare which bear no traces of his touch is a theory to the full as absurd as that which would impute to Shakespeare the charge of their entire composition.

The revolution effected by Marlowe naturally raised the same cry against its author as the revolution effected by Hugo. That Shakespeare should not at once have enlisted under his banner is less inexplicable than it may seem. He was naturally addicted to rhyme, though if we put aside the Sonnets we must admit that in rhyme he never did anything worth Marlowe's *Hero and Leander:* he did not, like Marlowe, see at once that it must be reserved for less active forms of poetry than the tragic drama; and he was personally, it seems, in opposition to Marlowe and his school of academic playwrights—the band of bards in which Oxford and Cambridge were respectively and so respectably represented by Peele and Greene. But in his very first plays, comic or tragic or historic, we can see the collision and conflict of the two influences; his evil angel, rhyme, yielding step by step and note by note to the strong advance of that better genius who came to lead him into the loftier path of Marlowe. There is not a single passage in *Titus Andronicus* more Shakespearean than the magnificent quatrain of Tamora upon the eagle and the little birds; but the rest of the scene in which we come upon it, and the whole scene preceding, are in blank verse of more variety and vigour than we find in the baser parts of the play; and these if any scenes we may surely attribute to Shakespeare. Again, the last battle of Talbot seems to me as undeniably the master's work as the scene in the Temple Gardens or the courtship of Margaret by Suffolk; this latter indeed, full as it is of natural and vivid grace, may perhaps not be beyond the highest reach of one or two among the rivals of his earliest years of work; while as we are certain that he cannot have written the opening scene, that he was at any stage of his career incapable of it, so may we believe as well as hope that he is guiltless of any complicity in that detestable part of the play which attempts to defile the memory of the virgin saviour of her country. [Note 1: One thing is certain: that damnable last scene at which the gorge rises even to remember it is in execution as unlike the crudest phase of Shakespeare's style as in conception it is unlike the idlest birth of his spirit. Let us hope that so foul a thing could not have been done in even tolerably good verse.] In style it is not, I think, above the range of George Peele at his best: and to have written even the last of those scenes can add but little discredit to the memory of a man already disgraced as the defamer of Eleanor of Castile; while it would be a relief to feel assured that there was but one English poet of any genius who could be capable of either villainy.

In this play, then, more decisively than in ***Titus Andronicus,*** we find Shakespeare at work (so to speak) with both hands—with his left hand of rhyme, and his right hand of blank verse. The left is loth to forego the practice of its peculiar music; yet as the action of the right grows freer and its touch grows stronger, it becomes more and more certain that the other must cease playing, under pain of producing mere discord and disturbance in the scheme of tragic harmony. We imagine that the writer must himself have felt the scene of the roses to be pitched in a truer key than the noble scene of parting between the old hero and his son on the verge of desperate battle and certain death. This is the last and loftiest farewell note of rhyming tragedy; still, in ***King Richard II*** and in ***Romeo and Juliet*** it struggles for awhile to keep its footing, but now more visibly in vain. The rhymed scenes in these plays are too plainly the survivals of a ruder and feebler stage of work; they cannot hold their own in the new order with even such discordant effect of incongruous excellence and inharmonious beauty as belongs to the death-scene of the Talbots when matched against the quarrelling scene of Somerset and York. Yet the briefest glance over the plays of the first epoch in the work of Shakespeare will suffice to show how protracted was the struggle and how gradual the defeat of rhyme. Setting aside the retouched plays, we find on the list one tragedy, two histories, and four if not five comedies, which the least critical reader would attribute to this first epoch of work. In three of these comedies rhyme can hardly be said to be beaten; that is, the rhyming scenes are on the whole equal to the unrhymed in power and beauty.

In the single tragedy, and in one of the two histories, we may say that rhyme fights hard for life, but is undeniably worsted; that is, they contain as to quantity a large proportion of rhymed verse, but as to quality the rhymed part bears no proportion whatever to the unrhymed. In two scenes we may say that the whole heart or spirit of ***Romeo and Juliet*** is summed up and distilled into perfect and pure expression; and these two are written in blank verse of equable and blameless melody. Outside the garden scene in the second act and the balcony scene in the third, there is much that is fanciful and graceful, much of elegiac pathos and fervid if fantastic passion; much also of superfluous rhetoric and (as it were) of wordy melody, which flows and foams hither and thither into something of extravagance and excess; but in these two there is no flaw, no outbreak, no superflux, and no failure. Throughout certain scenes of the third and fourth acts I think it may be reasonably and reverently allowed that the river of verse has broken its banks, not as yet through the force and weight of its gathering stream, but merely through the weakness of the barriers or boundaries found insufficient to confine it. And here we may with deference venture on a guess why Shakespeare was so long so loth to forego the restraint of rhyme. When he wrote, and even when he rewrote or at least retouched, his youngest tragedy he had not yet strength to walk straight in the steps of the mighty master, but two months older than himself by birth, whose foot never from the first faltered in the arduous path of severer tragic verse. The loveliest of love-plays is after all a child of "his salad days, when he was green in judgment," though assuredly not "cold in blood"—a physical condition as difficult to conceive of Shakespeare at any age as of Cleopatra. It is in the scenes of vehement passion, of ardour and of agony, that we feel the comparative weakness of a yet ungrown hand, the tentative uncertain grasp of a stripling giant The two utterly beautiful scenes are not of this kind; they deal with simple joy and "with simple sorrow, with the gladness of meeting and the sadness of parting love; but between and behind them come scenes of more fierce emotion, full of surprise, of violence, of unrest; and with these the poet is not yet (if I dare say so) quite strong enough to deal. Apollo has not yet put on the sinews of Hercules. At a later date we may fancy or may find that when the Herculean muscle is full-grown the voice in him which was as the voice of Apollo is for a passing moment impaired. In ***Measure far Measure,*** where the adult and gigantic god has grappled with the greatest and most terrible of energies and of passions, we miss the music of a younger note that rang through ***Romeo and Juliet;*** but before the end this too revives, as pure, as sweet, as fresh, but richer now and deeper than its first clear notes of the morning, in the heavenly harmony of ***Cymbeline*** and the ***Tempest.***

The same effusion or effervescence of words is perceptible in ***King Richard II.*** as in the greater (and the less good) part of ***Romeo and Juliet;*** and not less perceptible is the perpetual inclination of the poet to revert for help to rhyme, to hark back in search of support towards the half-forsaken habits of his poetic nonage. Feeling his foothold insecure on the hard and high ascent of the steeps of rhymeless verse, he stops and slips back ever and anon towards the smooth and marshy meadow whence he has hardly begun to climb. Any student who should wish to examine the conditions of the struggle at its height may be content to analyse the first act of this the first historical play of Shakespeare. As the tragedy moves onward, and the style gathers strength while the action gathers speed,—as (to borrow the phrase so admirably applied by Coleridge to Dryden) the poet's chariot-wheels get hot by driving fast,—the temptation of rhyme grows weaker, and the hand grows firmer which before lacked strength to wave it off. The one thing wholly or greatly admirable in this play is the exposition of the somewhat pitiful but not unpitiable character of King Richard. Among the scenes devoted to this exposition I of course include the whole of the death-scene of Gaunt, as well the part which precedes as the part which follows the actual appearance of his nephew on the stage; and into these scenes the intrusion of rhyme is rare and brief. They are written almost wholly in pure and fluent rather than vigorous or various blank verse; though I cannot discern in any of them an equality in power and passion to the magnificent scene of abdication in Marlowe's ***Edward II.*** This play, I think, must undoubtedly be regarded as the immediate model of Shakespeare's; and the comparison is one of inexhaustible interest to all students of dramatic poetry. To the highest height of the earlier master I do not think that the mightier poet who was as yet in great measure his pupil has ever risen in this the first (as I take it) of his historic plays. Of composition and proportion he has perhaps already a somewhat better idea. But in grasp of character, always excepting the one central figure of the piece, we find his hand as yet the unsteadier of the two. Even after a lifelong study of this as of all other plays of Shakespeare, it is for me at least impossible to determine what I doubt if the poet could himself have clearly defined—the main principle, the motive and the meaning of such characters as York, Norfolk, and Aumerle. The Gaveston and the Mortimer of Marlowe are far more solid and definite figures than these; yet none after that of Richard is more important to the scheme of Shakespeare. They are fitful, shifting, vaporous: their outlines change, withdraw, dissolve, and "leave not a rack behind." They, not Antony, are like the clouds of evening described in the most glorious of so many glorious passages put long afterwards by Shakespeare into the mouth of his latest Roman hero. They "cannot hold this visible shape" in which the poet at first presents them even long enough to leave a distinct image, a decisive impression for better or for worse, upon the mind's eye of the most simple arid open-hearted reader. They are ghosts, not men; ***simulacra modis pallentia miris.*** You cannot descry so much as the original intention of the artist's hand which began to draw and relaxed its hold of the brush before the first lines were fairly traced. And in the last, the worst and weakest scene of all, in which York pleads with Bolingbroke for the death of the son whose mother pleads against her husband for his life, there is a final relapse into rhyme and rhyming epigram, into the "jigging vein" dried up (we might have hoped) long since by the very glance of Marlowe's Apollonian scorn. It would be easy, agreeable, and irrational to ascribe without further evidence than its badness this misconceived and misshapen scene to some other hand than Shakespeare's. It is below the weakest, the rudest, the hastiest scene attributable to Marlowe; it is false, wrong, artificial beyond the worst of his bad and boyish work; but it has a certain likeness for the worse to the crudest work of Shakespeare. It is difficult to say to what, depths of bad taste the writer of certain passages in ***Venus and Adonis*** could not fall before his genius or his judgment was full-grown. To invent an earlier play on the subject and imagine this scene a surviving fragment, a floating waif of that imaginary wreck, would in my opinion be an uncritical mode of evading the question at issue. It must be regarded as the last hysterical struggle of rhyme to maintain its place in tragedy; and the explanation, I would fain say the excuse, of its reappearance may perhaps be simply this; that the poet was not yet dramatist enough to feel for each of his characters an equal or proportionate regard; to divide and disperse his interest among the various crowd of figures which claim each in its place, and each after its kind, a fair and adequate share of their creator's attention and sympathy. His present interest was here wholly concentrated on the single figure of Richard; and when that for the time was absent, the subordinate figures became to him but heavy and vexatious encumbrances, to be shifted on and off the stage with as much of haste and as little of labour as might be possible to an impatient and uncertain hand. Now all tragic poets, I presume, from Æschylus the godlike father of them all to the last aspirant who may struggle after the traces of his steps, have been poets before they were tragedians; their lips have had power to sing before their feet had strength to tread the stage, before their hands had skill to paint or carve figures from the life. With Shakespeare it was so as certainly as with Shelley, as evidently as with Hugo. It is in the great comic poets, in Molière and in Congreve, [Note 1: It is not the least of Lord Macaulay's offences against art that he should have contributed the temporary weight of his influence as a critic to the support of so ignorant and absurd a tradition of criticism as that which classes the great writer here mentioned with the brutal if "brawny" Wycherley—a classification almost to be paralleled with that which in the days of our fathers saw fit to couple together the names of Balzac and of Sue. Any competent critic will always recognise in *The Way of the World* one of the glories, in *The Country Wife* one of the disgraces, of dramatic and of English literature. The stains discernible on the masterpiece of Congreve are trivial and conventional; the mere conception of the other man's work displays a mind so prurient and leprous, uncovers such an unfathomable and unimaginable beastliness of imagination, that in the present age at least he would probably have figured as a virtuous journalist and professional rebuker of poetic vice or artistic aberration.] our; own lesser Molière so far inferior in breadth and depth, in tenderness and strength, to the greatest writer of the "great age," yet so near him in science and in skill, so like him in brilliance and in force,—it is in these that we find theatrical instinct twin-born with imaginative impulse, dramatic power with inventive perception.

In the second historic play which can be wholly ascribed to Shakespeare we still find the poetic or rhetorical quality for the most part in excess of the dramatic; but in *King Richard III.* the bonds of rhyme at least are fairly broken. This only of all Shakespeare's plays belongs absolutely to the school of Marlowe. The influence of the elder master, and that influence alone, is perceptible from end to end. Here at last we can see that Shakespeare has decidedly chosen his side. It is as fiery in passion, as single in purpose, as rhetorical often though never so inflated in expression, as *Tamburlaine* itself. It is doubtless a better piece of work than Marlowe ever did; I dare not say, than Marlowe ever could have done. It is not for any man to measure, above all is it not for any workman in the field of tragic poetry lightly to take on himself the responsibility or the authority to pronounce, what it is that Christopher Marlowe could not have done; but, dying as he did and when he did, it is certain that he has not left us a work so generally and so variously admirable as ***King Richard III.*** As certain is it that but for him this play could never have been written. At a later date the subject would have been handled otherwise, had the poet chosen to handle it at all; and in his youth he could not have treated it as he has without the guidance and example of Marlowe. Not only are its highest qualities of energy, of exuberance, of pure and lofty style, of sonorous and successive harmonies, the very qualities that never fail to distinguish those first dramatic models which were fashioned by his ardent hand; the strenuous and single-handed grasp of character, the motion and action of combining and contending powers, which here for the first time we find sustained with equal and unfaltering vigour throughout the length of a whole play, we perceive, though imperfectly, in the work of Marlowe before we can trace them even as latent or infant forces in the work of Shakespeare.

In the exquisite and delightful comedies of his earliest period we can hardly discern any sign, any promise of them at all. One only of these, the ***Comedy of Errors,*** has in it anything of dramatic composition and movement; and what it has of these, I need hardly remind the most cursory of students, is due by no means to Shakespeare. What is due to him, and to him alone, is the honour of having embroidered on the naked old canvas of comic action those flowers of elegiac beauty which vivify and diversify the scene of Plautus as reproduced by the art of Shakespeare. In the next generation so noble a poet as Rotrou, whom perhaps it might not be inaccurate to call the French Marlowe, and who had (what Marlowe had not) the gift of comic as well as of tragic excellence, found nothing of this kind and little of any kind to add to the old poet's admirable but arid sketch of farcical incident or accident. But in this light and lovely work of. the youth of Shakespeare we find for the first time that strange and sweet admixture of farce with fancy, of lyric charm with comic effect, which recurs so often in his later work, from the date of *As You Like It* to the date of the *Winter's Tale,* and which no later poet had ventured to recombine in the same play till our own time had given us, in the author of *Tragaldabas,* one who could alternate without, confusing the woodland courtship of Eliseo and Caprina with the tavern braggardism of Grif and Minotoro. The sweetness and simplicity of lyric or elegiac loveliness which fill and inform the scenes where Adriana, her sister, and the Syracusan Antipholus exchange the expression of their errors and their loves, belong to Shakespeare alone; and may help us to understand how the young poet who at the outset of his divine career had struck into this fresh untrodden path of poetic comedy should have been, as we have seen that he was, loth to learn from another and an alien teacher the hard and necessary lesson that this flowery path would never lead him towards the loftier land of tragic poetry. For as yet, even in the nominally or intentionally tragic and historic work of the first period, we descry always and everywhere and still preponderant the lyric element, the fantastic element, or even the elegiac element. All these queens and heroines of history and tragedy have rather an Ovidian than a Sophoclean grace of bearing and of speech.

The example afforded by the ***Comedy of Errors*** would suffice to show that rhyme, however inadequate for tragic use, is by no means a bad instrument for romantic comedy. In another of Shakespeare's earliest works, which might almost be described as a lyrical farce, rhyme plays also a great part; but the finest passage, the real crown and flower of *Love's Labour's Lost,* is the praise or apology of love spoken by Biron in blank verse. This is worthy of Marlowe for dignity and sweetness, but has also the grace of a light and radiant fancy enamoured of itself, begotten between thought and mirth, a child-god with grave lips and laughing eyes, whose inspiration is nothing akin to Marlowe's. In this as in the overture of the play and in its closing scene, but especially in the noble passage which winds up for a year the courtship of Biron and Rosaline, the spirit which informs the speech of the poet is finer of touch and deeper of tone than in the sweetest of the serious interludes of the ***Comedy of Errors.*** The play is in the main a yet lighter thing, and more wayward and capricious in build, more formless and fantastic in plot, more incomposite altogether than that first heir of Shakespeare's comic invention, which on its own ground is perfect in its consistency, blameless in composition and coherence; while in *Love's Labour's Lost* the fancy for the most part runs wild as the wind, and the structure of the story is as that of a house of clouds which the wind builds and unbuilds at pleasure. Here we find a very riot of rhymes, wild and wanton in their half-grown grace as a troop of "young satyrs, tender-hoofed and ruddy-horned"; during certain scenes we seem almost to stand again by the cradle of new-born comedy, and hear the first lisping and laughing accents run over from her baby lips in bubbling rhyme; but when the note changes we recognise the speech of gods. For the first time in our literature the higher key of poetic or romantic comedy is finely touched to a fine issue. The divine instrument fashioned by Marlowe for tragic purposes alone has found at once its new sweet use in the hands of Shakespeare. The way is prepared for *As You Like It* and the *Tempest;* the language is discovered which will befit the lips of Rosalind and Miranda.

What was highest as poetry in the *Comedy of Errors* was mainly in rhyme; all indeed, we might say, between the prelude spoken by Ægeon and the appearance in the last scene of his wife: in *Love's Labour's Lost* what was highest was couched wholly in blank verse; in the *Two Gentlemen of Verona* rhyme has fallen seemingly into abeyance, and there are no passages of such elegiac beauty as in the former, of such exalted eloquence sis in the latter of these plays; there is an even sweetness, a simple equality of grace in thought and language which keeps the whole poem in tune, written as it is in a subdued key of unambitious harmony. In perfect unity and keeping the composition of this beautiful sketch may perhaps be said to mark a stage of advance, a new point of work attained, a faint but sensible change of manner, signalised by increased firmness of hand and clearness of outline. Slight and swift in execution as it is, few and simple as are the chords here struck of character and emotion, every shade of drawing and every note of sound is at one with the whole scheme of form and music. Here too is the first dawn of that higher and more tender humour which was never given in such perfection to any man as ultimately to Shakespeare; one touch of the by-play of Launce and his immortal dog is worth all the bright fantastic interludes of Boyet and Adriano, Costard and Holofernes; worth even half the sallies of Mercutio, and half the dancing doggrel or broad-witted prose of either Dromio. But in the final poem which concludes and crowns the first epoch of Shakespeare's work, the special graces and peculiar glories of each that went before are gathered together as in one garland "of every hue and every scent" The young genius of the master of all our poets finds its consummation in the ***Midsummer Night's Dream.*** The blank verse is as full, sweet, and strong as the best of Biron's or Romeo's; the rhymed verse as clear, pure, and true as the simplest and truest melody of ***Venus and Adonis*** or the ***Comedy of Errors.*** But here each kind of excellence is equal throughout; there are here no purple patches on a gown of serge, but one seamless and imperial robe of a single dye. Of the lyric or the prosaic part, the counterchange of loves and laughters, of fancy fine as air and imagination high as heaven, what need can there be for any one to shame himself by the helpless attempt to say some word not utterly unworthy? Let it suffice us to accept this poem as the landmark of our first stage, and pause to look back from it on what lies behind us of partial or of perfect work.

The highest point attained in this first period lies in the domain of comedy or romance, and belongs as much to lyric as to dramatic poetry; its sovereign quality is that of sweetness and springtide of fairy fancy crossed with light laughter and light trouble that end in perfect music. In history as in tragedy the master's hand has not yet come to its full strength and skill; its touch is not yet wholly assured, its work not yet wholly blameless. Besides the plays undoubtedly and entirely due to the still growing genius of Shakespeare, we have taken note but of two among those which bear the partial imprint of his hand. The long-vexed question as to the authorship of the latter parts of ***King Henry VI.,*** in their earlier or later form, has not been touched upon; nor do I design to reopen that perpetual source of debate unstanchable and inexhaustible dispute by any length of scrutiny or inquisition of detail. Two points must of course be taken for granted: that Marlowe was more or less concerned in the production, and Shakespeare in the revision of these plays; whether before or after his additions to the original ***First Part of King Henry VI.*** we cannot determine, though the absence of rhyme might seem to indicate a later date for the recast of the ***Contention.*** But it is noticeable that the style of Marlowe appears more vividly and distinctly in passages of the reformed than of the unreformed plays. Those famous lines, for example, which open the fourth act of the ***Second Part of King Henry VI.,*** are not to be found in the corresponding scene of the first part of the *Contention;* yet, whether they belong to the original sketch of the play, or were inserted as an afterthought into the revised and expanded copy, the authorship of these verses is surely unmistakable:—

> The gaudy, blabbing, and remorseful day
> Is crept into the bosom of the sea;
> And now loud howling wolves arouse the jades
> That drag the tragic melancholy night, etc.

Aut Christophorus Marlowe, aut diabolus; it is inconceivable that any imitator but one should have had the power so to catch the very trick of his hand, the very note of his voice, and incredible that the one who might would have set himself to do so: for if this be not indeed the voice and this the hand of Marlowe, then what we find in these verses is not the fidelity of a follower, but the servility of a copyist. No parasitic rhymester of past or present days who feeds his starveling talent on the shreds and orts, "the fragments, scraps, the bits and greasy relics "of another man's board, ever uttered a more parrot-like note of plagiary. The very exactitude of the repetition is a strong argument against the theory which attributes it to Shakespeare. That he had much at starting to learn of Marlowe, and that he did learn much—that in his earliest plays, and above all in his earliest historic plays, the influence of the elder poet, the echo of his style, the iteration of his manner, may perpetually be traced—I have already shown that I should be the last to question; but so exact an echo, so servile an iteration as this, I believe we shall nowhere find in them. The sonorous accumulation of emphatic epithets—as in the magnificent first verse of this passage—is indeed at least as much a note of the young Shakespeare's style as of his master's; but even were this one verse less in the manner of the elder than the younger poet—and this we can hardly say that it is—no single verse detached from its context can weigh a feather against the full and flawless evidence of the whole speech. And of all this there is nothing in the *Contention;* the scene there opens in bald and flat nakedness of prose, striking at once into the immediate matter of stage business without the decoration of a passing epithet or a single trope.

From this sample it might seem that the main difficulty must be to detect anywhere the sign-manual of Shakespeare, even in the best passages of the revised play. On the other hand, it has not unreasonably been maintained that even in the next scene of this same act in its original form, and in all those following which treat of Cade's insurrection, there is evidence of such qualities as can hardly be ascribed to any hand then known but Shakespeare's. The forcible realism, the simple vigour and lifelike humour of these scenes, cannot, it is urged, be due to any other so early at work in the field of comedy. A critic desirous to press this point might further insist on the likeness or identity of tone between these and all later scenes in which Shakespeare has taken on him to paint the action and passion of an insurgent populace. With him, it might too plausibly be argued, the people once risen in revolt for any just or unjust cause is always the mob, the unwashed rabble, the swinish multitude; full as he is of wise and gracious tenderness for individual character, of swift and ardent pity for personal suffering, he has no deeper or finer feeling than scorn for "the beast with many heads" that fawn and butt at bidding as they are swayed by the vain and violent breath of any worthless herdsman. For the drovers who guide and misguide at will the turbulent flocks of their mutinous cattle his store of bitter words is inexhaustible; it is a treasure-house of obloquy which can never be drained dry. All this, or nearly all this, we must admit; but it brings us no nearer to any but a floating and conjectural kind of solution. In the earliest form known to us of this play it should seem that we have traces of Shakespeare's handiwork, in the latest that we find evidence of Marlowe's. But it would be something too extravagant for the veriest wind-sucker among commentators to start a theory that a revision was made of his original work by Marlowe after additions had been made to it by Shakespeare; yet we have seen that the most unmistakable signs of Marlowe's handiwork, the passages which show most plainly the personal and present seal of his genius, belong to the play only in its revised form; while there is no part of the whole composition which can so confidently be assigned to Shakespeare as to the one man then capable of such work, as can an entire and important episode of the play in its unrevised state. Now the proposition that Shakespeare was the sole author of both plays in their earliest extant shape is refuted at once and equally from without and from within, by evidence of tradition and by evidence of style. There is therefore proof irresistible and unmistakable of at least a double authorship; and the one reasonable conclusion left to us would seem to be this; that the first edition we possess of these plays is a partial transcript of the text as it stood after the first additions had been made by Shakespeare to the original work of Marlowe and others; for that this original was the work of more hands than one, and hands of notably unequal power, we have again the united witness of traditional and internal evidence to warrant our belief: and that among the omissions of this imperfect text were certain passages of the original work, which were ultimately restored in the final revision of the entire poem as it now stands among the collected works of Shakespeare.

No competent critic who has given due study to the genius of Marlowe will admit that there is a single passage of tragic or poetic interest in either form of the text, which is beyond the reach of the father of English tragedy: or, if there be one seeming exception in the expanded and transfigured version of Clifford's monologue over his father's corpse, which is certainly more in Shakespeare's tragic manner than in Marlowe's, and the style of a later period than that in which he was on the whole apparently content to reproduce or to emulate the tragic manner of Marlowe, there is at least but this one exception to the general and absolute truth of the rule; and even this great tragic passage is rather out of the range of Marlowe's style than beyond the scope of his genius. In the later as in the earlier version of these plays, the one manifest excellence of which we have no reason to suppose him capable is manifest in the comic or prosaic scenes alone. The first great rapid sketch of the dying cardinal, afterwards so nobly enlarged and perfected on revision by the same or by a second artist, is as clearly within the capacity of Marlowe as of Shakespeare; and in either edition of the latter play, successively known as ***The True Tragedy of Richard Duke of York,*** as the ***Second Part of the Contention,*** and as the ***Third Part of King Henry VI.,*** the dominant figure which darkens all the close of the poem with presage of a direr day is drawn by the same strong hand in the same tragic outline. From the first to the last stage of the work there is no mark of change or progress here; the whole play indeed has undergone less revision, as it certainly needed less, than the preceding part of the ***Contention.*** Those great verses which resume the whole spirit of Shakespeare's Richard—finer perhaps in themselves than any passage of the play which bears his name—are wellnigh identical in either form of the poem; but the reviser, with admirable judgment, has struck out, whether from his own text or that of another, the line which precedes them in the original sketch, where the passage runs thus:—

I had no father, I am like no father;
I have no brothers, I am like no brother;

(this reiteration is exactly in the first manner of our tragic drama;)

And this word love, which greybeards term divine, etc.

It would be an impertinence to transcribe the rest of a passage which rings in the ear of every reader's memory; but it may be noted that the erasure by which its effect is so singularly heightened with the inborn skill of so divine an instinct is just such an alteration as would be equally likely to occur to the original writer on glancing over his printed text or to a poet of kindred power, who, while busied in retouching and filling out the sketch of his predecessor, might be struck by the opening for so great an improvement at so small a cost of suppression. My own conjecture would incline to the belief that we have here a perfect example of the manner in which Shakespeare may be presumed, when such a task was set before him, to have dealt with the text of Marlowe. That at the outset of his career he was so employed, as well as on the texts of lesser poets, we have on all hands as good evidence of every kind as can be desired; proof on one side from the text of the revised plays, which are as certainly in part the work of his hand as they are in part the work of another; and proof on the opposite side from the open and clamorous charge of his rivals, whose imputations can be made to bear no reasonable meaning but this by the most violent ingenuity of perversion, and who presumably were not persons of such frank imbecility, such innocent and infantine malevolence, as to forge against their most dangerous enemy the pointless and edgeless weapon of a charge which, if ungrounded, must have been easier to refute than to devise. Assuming then that in common with other young poets of his day he was thus engaged during the first years of his connection with the stage, we should naturally have expected to find him handling the text of Marlowe with more of reverence and less o freedom than that of meaner men: ready, as in the **Contention,** to clear away with no timid hand their weaker and more inefficient work, to cancel and supplant it by worthier matter of his own; but when occupied in recasting the verse of Marlowe, not less ready to confine his labour to such slight and skilful strokes of art as that which has led us into this byway of speculation; to the correction of a false note, the addition of a finer touch, the perfection of a meaning half expressed or a tone of half-uttered music; to the invigoration of sense and metre by substitution of the right word for the wrong, of a fuller phrase for one feebler; to the excision of such archaic and superfluous repetitions as are signs of a cruder stage of workmanship, relics of a ruder period of style, survivals of the earliest form or habit of dramatic poetry. Such work as this, however humble in our present eyes, which look before and after, would assuredly have been worthy of the workman and his task; an office no less fruitful of profit, and no more unbeseeming the pupil hand of the future master, than the subordinate handiwork of the young Raffaelle or Leonardo on the canvas of Verrocchio or Perugino.

Of the doubtful or spurious plays which have been with more or less show of reason ascribed to this first period of Shakespeare's art, I have here no more to say than that I purpose in the proper place to take account of the only two among them which bear the slightest trace of any possible touch of his hand. For these two there is not, as it happens, the least witness of tradition or outward likelihood which might warrant us in assigning them a place apart from the rest, and nearer the chance of reception into the rank that has been claimed for them; while those plays in whose favour there is some apparent evidence from without, such as the fact of early or even original attribution to the master's hand, are, with one possible exception, utterly beyond the pale of human consideration as at any stage whatever the conceivable work of Shakespeare.

Considering that his two attempts at narrative or rather semi-narrative and semi-reflective poetry belong obviously to an early stage of his earliest period, we may rather here than elsewhere take notice that there are some curious points of coincidence for evil as for good between the fortunes of Shakespeare's plays and the fortunes of his poems. In either case we find that some part at least of his earlier and inferior work has fared better at the blind hands of chance and the brutish hands of printers than some part at least of his riper and more precious products. His two early poems would seem to have had the good hap of his personal supervision in their passage through the press. Upon them, at least since the time of Coleridge, who as usual has said on this subject the first and the last word that need be said, it seems to me that fully sufficient notice and fully adequate examination have been expended; and that nothing at once new and true can now be profitably said in praise or in dispraise of them. Of **A Lovers Complaint,** marked as it is throughout with every possible sign suggestive of a far later date and a far different inspiration, I have only space or need to remark that it contains two of the most exquisitely Shakespearean verses ever vouchsafed to us by Shakespeare, and two of the most execrably euphuistic or dysphuistic lines ever inflicted on us by man. Upon the Sonnets such a preposterous pyramid of presumptuous commentary has long since been reared by the Cimmerian speculation and Bœotian "brain-sweat" of sciolists and scholiasts, that no modest man will hope and no wise man will desire to add to the structure or subtract from it one single brick of proof or disproof, theorem or theory. As yet the one contemporary book which has ever been supposed to throw any direct or indirect light on the mystic matter remains as inaccessible and unhelpful to students as though it had never been published fifteen years earlier than the date of their publication and four years before the book in which Meres notices the circulation of Shakespeare's "sugared sonnets among his private friends." It would be a most noble and thankworthy addition to a list of labours beyond praise and benefits beyond price, if my honoured friend Dr. Grosart could find the means to put a crown upon the achievements of his learning and a seal upon the obligations of our gratitude by the one inestimable boon long hoped for against hoping, and as yet but "a vision in a dream" to the most learned and most loving of true Shakespearean students; by the issue or reissue in its full and perfect likeness, collated at last and complete, of **Willobie his A visa.** [Note 1: Since this passage first went to press, I have received from Dr. Grosart the most happy news that he has procured a perfect copy of this precious volume, and will shortly add it to his occasional issues of golden waifs and strays forgotten by the ebb-tide of time. Not even the disinterment of Robert Chester's "glorified" poem, with its appended jewels of verse from Shakespeare's very hand and from others only less great than Shakespeare's, all now at last reset in their strange original framework, was a gift of greater price than this.]

It was long since more than time that the worthless and impudent imposture called *The Passionate Pilgrim* should be exposed and expelled from its station at the far end of Shakespeare's poems. What Coleridge said of Ben Jonson's epithet for "turtle-footed peace," we may say of the label affixed to this rag-picker's bag of stolen goods: *The Passionate Pilgrim* is a pretty title, a very pretty title; pray what may it mean? In all the larcenous little bundle of verse there is neither a poem which bears that name nor a poem by which that name would be bearable. The publisher of the booklet was like "one Ragozine, a most notorious pirate"; and the method no less than the motive of his rascality in the present instance is palpable and simple enough. Fired by the immediate and instantly proverbial popularity of Shakespeare's *Venus and Adonis,* he hired, we may suppose, some ready hack of unclean hand to supply him with three doggrel sonnets on the same subject, noticeable only for their porcine quality of prurience: he procured by some means a rough copy or an incorrect transcript of two genuine and unpublished sonnets by Shakespeare, which with the acute instinct of a felonious tradesman he laid atop of his worthless wares by way of gilding to their base metal: he stole from the two years published text of *Love's Labour's Lost,* and reproduced with more or less mutilation or corruption, the sonnet of Longavile, the "canzonet" of Biron, and the far lovelier love-song of Dumaine. The rest of the ragman's gatherings, with three most notable exceptions, is little better for the most part than dry rubbish or disgusting refuse; unless a plea may haply be put in for the pretty commonplaces of the lines on a "sweet rose, fair flower," and so forth; for the couple of thin and pallid if tender and tolerable copies of verse on "Beauty" and "Good Night," or the passably light and lively stray of song on "crabbed age and youth." I need not say that those three exceptions are the stolen and garbled work of Marlowe and of Barnfield, our elder Shelley and our first-born Keats; the singer of Cynthia in verse well worthy of Endymion, who would seem to have died as a poet in the same fatal year of his age that Keats died as a man; the first adequate English laureate of the nightingale, to be supplanted or equalled by none until the advent of his mightier brother.

II.

THE second period is that of perfection in comic and historic style. The final heights and depths of tragedy, with all its reach of thought and all its pulse of passion, are yet to be scaled and sounded; but to this stage belongs the special quality of faultless, joyous, facile command upon each faculty required of the presiding genius for service. or for sport. It is in the middle period of his work that the language of Shakespeare is most limpid in its fullness, the style most pure, the thought most transparent through the close and luminous raiment of perfect expression. The conceits and crudities of the first stage are outgrown and cast aside; the harshness and obscurity which at times may strike us as among the notes of his third manner have as yet no place in the flawless work of this second stage. That which has to be said is not yet too great for perfection of utterance; passion has not yet grappled with thought in so close and fierce an embrace as to strain and rend the garment of words, though stronger and subtler than ever was woven of human speech. Neither in his first nor in his last stage would the style of Shakespeare, even were it possible by study to reproduce it, be of itself a perfect and blameless model; but his middle style, that in which the typical plays of his second period are written, would be, if it were possible to imitate, the most absolute pattern that could be set before man. I do not speak of mere copyist's work, the parasitic knack of retailing cast phrases, tricks and turns of accent, cadences and catchwords proper only to the natural manner of the man who first came by instinct upon them, and by instinct put them to use; I speak of that faithful and fruitful discipleship of love with which the highest among poets and the I; most original among workmen have naturally been always the first to study and the most earnest to follow the footsteps of their greatest precursors in that kind. And this only high and profitable form of study and discipleship can set before itself, even in the work of Shakespeare, no pattern so perfect, no model so absolute, as is afforded by the style or manner of his second period.

To this stage belong by spiritual right if not by material, by rule of poetic order if not by date of actual succession, the greatest of his English histories and four of his greatest and most perfect comedies; the four greatest we might properly call them, reserving for another class the last divine triad of romantic plays which it is alike inaccurate to number among tragedies or comedies proper: the *Winter's Tale, Cymbeline,* and the *Tempest,* which belong of course wholly to his last manner, or, if accuracy must be strained even to pedantry, to the second manner of his third or final stage. A single masterpiece which may be classed either among histories or tragedies belongs to the middle period; and to this also we must refer, if not the ultimate form, yet assuredly the first sketch at least of that which is commonly regarded as the typical and supreme work of Shakespeare. Three lesser comedies, one of them in great part the recast or rather the transfiguration of an earlier poet's work, complete the list of plays assignable to the second epoch of his genius.

The ripest fruit of historic or national drama, the consummation and the crown of Shakespeare's labours in that line, must of course be recognised and saluted by all students in the supreme and sovereign trilogy of *King Henry IV.* and *King Henry V.* On a lower degree only than this final and imperial work we find the two chronicle histories which remain to be classed. In style as in structure they bear witness of a power less perfect, a less impeccable hand. They have less of perceptible instinct, less of vivid and vigorous utterance; the breath of their inspiration is less continuous and less direct, the fashion of their eloquence is more deliberate and more prepense; there is more of study and structure apparent in their speech, and less in their general scheme of action. Of all Shakespeare's plays they are the most rhetorical; there is more talk than song in them, less poetry than oratory; more finish than form, less movement than incident. Scene is laid upon scene, and event succeeds event, as stone might be laid on stone and story might succeed story in a building reared by mere might of human handiwork; not as in a city or temple whose walls had risen of themselves to the lyric breath and stroke of a greater than Amphion; moulded out of music by no rule or line of mortal measure, with no sound of axe or anvil, but only of smitten strings: built by harp and not by hand.

The lordly structure of these poems is the work of a royal workman, full of masterdom and might, sublime in the state and strength of its many mansions, but less perfect in proportion and less aerial in build than the very highest fabrics fashioned after their own great will by the supreme architects of song. Of these plays, and of these alone among the maturer works of Shakespeare, it may be said that the best parts are discernible from the rest, divisible by analysis and separable by memory from the scenes which precede them or follow and the. Characters which surround them or succeed. Constance and Katherine rise up into remembrance apart from their environment and above it, stand clear in our minds of the crowded company with which the poet has begirt their central figures. In all other of his great tragic works,—even in **Hamlet,** if we have grace and sense to read it aright and not awry,—it is not of any single person or separate passage that we think when we speak of it; it is to the whole masterpiece that the mind turns at mention of its name. The one entire and perfect chrysolite of **Othello** is neither Othello nor Desdemona nor Iago but each and all; the play of **Hamlet** is more than Hamlet himself, the poem even here is too great to be resumed in the person. But Constance is the jewel of **King John,** and Katherine is the crowning blossom of **King Henry VIII.**—a funeral flower as of "marigolds on death-beds blowing," an opal of as pure water as "tears of perfect moan," with fitful fire at its heart, ominous of evil and sorrow, set in a mourning band of jet on the forefront of the poem, that the brow so circled may, "like to a title-leaf, foretell the nature of a tragic volume." Not indeed that without these the ground would in either case be barren; but that in either field our eye rests rather on these and other separate ears of wheat that overtop the ranks, than on the waving width of the whole harvest at once. In the one play our memory turns next to the figures of Arthur and the Bastard, in the other to those of Wolsey and his king: the residue in either case is made up of outlines more lightly and slightly drawn. In two scenes the figure of King John rises indeed to the highest height even of Shakespearean tragedy; for the rest of the play the lines of his character are cut no deeper, the features of his personality stand out in no sharper relief, than those of Eleanor or the French king; but the scene in which he tempts Hubert to the edge of the pit of hell sounds a deeper note and touches a subtler string in the tragic nature of man than had been struck by any poet save Dante alone, since the reign of the Greek tragedians. The cunning and profound simplicity of the few last weighty words which drop like flakes of poison that blister where they fall from the deadly lips of the king is a new quality in our tragic verse; there was no foretaste of such a thing in the passionate imagination which clothed itself in the mighty music of Marlowe's burning song. The elder master might indeed have written the magnificent speech which ushers in with gradual rhetoric and splendid reticence the black suggestion of a deed without a name; his hand might have woven with no less imperial skill the elaborate raiment of words and images which wraps up in fold upon fold, as with swaddling-bands of purple and golden embroidery, the shapeless and miscreated birth of a murderous purpose that labours into light even while it loathes the light and itself; but only Shakespeare could give us the first sample of that more secret and terrible knowledge which reveals itself in the brief heavy whispers that seal the commission and sign the warrant of the king. Webster alone of all our tragic poets has had strength to emulate in this darkest line of art the handiwork of his master. We find nowhere such an echo or reflection of the spirit of this scene as in the last tremendous dialogue of Bosola with Ferdinand in the house of murder and madness, while their spotted souls yet flutter between conscience and distraction, hovering for an hour as with broken wings on the confines of either province of hell. One pupil at least could put to this awful profit the study of so great a model; but with the single and sublime exception of that other design from the same great hand, which bares before us the mortal anguish of Bracciano, no copy or imitation of the scene in which John dies by poison has ever come near enough to evade the sentence it provokes. The shrill tremulous agony of Fletcher's Valentinian is to the sullen and slow death-pangs of Shakespeare's tyrant as the babble of a suckling to the accents of a man. As far beyond the reach of any but his maker's hand is the pattern of a perfect English warrior, set once for all before the eyes of all ages in the figure of the noble Bastard. The national side of Shakespeare's genius, the heroic vein of patriotism that runs like a thread of living fire through the world-wide range of his omnipresent spirit, has never, to my thinking, found vent or expression to such glorious purpose as here. Not even in Hotspur or Prince Hal has he mixed with more godlike sleight of hand all the lighter and graver good qualities of the national character, or compounded of them all so lovable a nature as this. In those others we admire and enjoy the same bright fiery temper of soul, the same buoyant and fearless mastery of fate or fortune, the same gladness and glory of life made lovely with all the labour and laughter of its full fresh days; but no quality of theirs binds our hearts to them as they are bound to Philip—not by his loyal valour, his keen young wit, his kindliness, constancy, readiness of service as swift and sure in the day of his master's bitterest shame and shamefullest trouble as in the blithest hour of battle and that first good fight which won back his father's spoils from his father's slayer; but more than all these, for that lightning of divine rage and pity, of tenderness that speaks in thunder and indignation that makes fire of its tears, in the horror of great compassion which falls on him, the tempest and storm of a beautiful and godlike anger which shakes his strength of spirit and bows his high heart down at sight of Arthur dead. Being thus, as he is, the English masterwork of Shakespeare's hand, we may well accept him as the best man known to us that England ever made; the hero that Nelson must have been had he never come too near Naples.

I am not minded to say much of Shakespeare's Arthur; there are one or two figures in the world of his work of which there are no words that would be fit or good to say. Another of these is Cordelia. The place they have in our lives and thoughts is not one for talk; the niche set apart for them to inhabit in our secret hearts is not penetrable by the lights and noises of common day. There are chapels in the cathedral of man's highest art as in that of his inmost life, not made to be set open to the eyes and feet of the world. Love and death and memory keep charge for us in silence of some beloved names. It is the crowning glory of genius, the final miracle and transcendant gift of poetry that it can add to the number of these, and engrave on the very heart of our remembrance fresh names and memories of its own creation.

There is one younger child in this heavenly family of Shakespeare's who sits side by side with Arthur in the secret places of our thought; there are but two or three that I remember among the children of other poets who may be named in the same year with them: as Fletcher's Hengo, Webster's Giovanni, and Landor's Cæsarion. Of this princely trinity of boys the "bud of Britain" is as yet the most famous flower; yet even in the broken words of childish heroism that falter on his dying lips there is nothing of more poignant pathos, more "dearly sweet and bitter," than Giovanni's talk of his dead mother and all her sleepless nights now ended for ever in a sleep beyond tears or dreams. Perhaps the most nearly faultless in finish and proportion of perfect nature among all the noble three is Landor's portrait of the imperial and right Roman child of Cæsar and Cleopatra. I know not but this may be found in the judgment of men to come wellnigh the most pathetic and heroic figure bequeathed us after more than eighty years of a glorious life by the indomitable genius of our own last Roman and republican poet.

We have come now to that point at the opening of the second stage in his work where the supreme genius of all time begins first to meddle with the mysteries and varieties of human character, to handle its finer and more subtle qualities, to harmonise its more untuned and jarring discords; giving here and thus the first proof of a power never shared in like measure by the mightiest among the sons of men, a sovereign and serene capacity to fathom the else unfathomable depths of spiritual nature, to solve its else insoluble riddles, to reconcile its else irreconcilable discrepancies. In his first stage Shakespeare had dropped his plummet no deeper into the sea of the spirit of man than Marlowe had sounded before him; and in the channel of simple emotion no poet could cast surer line with steadier hand than he. Further down in the dark and fiery depths of human pain and mortal passion no soul could search than his who first rendered into speech the aspirations and the agonies of a ruined and revolted spirit And until Shakespeare found in himself the strength of eyesight to read and the cunning of handiwork to render those wider diversities of emotion and those further complexities of character which lay outside the range of Marlowe, he certainly cannot be said to have outrun the winged feet, outstripped the fiery flight of his forerunner. In the heaven of our tragic song the first-born star on the forehead of its herald god was not outshone till the full midsummer meridian of that greater godhead before whom he was sent to prepare a pathway for the sun. Through all the forenoon of our triumphant day, till the utter consummation and ultimate ascension of dramatic poetry incarnate and transfigured in the master-singer of the world, the quality of his tragedy was as that Marlowe's, broad, single, and intense; large of hand, voluble of tongue, direct of purpose. With the dawn of its latter epoch a new power comes upon it, to find clothing and expression in new forms of speech and after a new style. The language has put off its foreign decorations of lyric and elegiac ornament; it has found already its infinite gain in the loss of those sweet superfluous graces which encumbered the march and enchain the utterance of its childhood. The figures which it invests are now no more the types of a sing passion, the incarnations of a single thought. The now demand a scrutiny which tests the power a mind and tries the value of a judgment; they appeal to something more than the instant apprehension which sufficed to respond to the immediately claim of those that went before them. Romeo an Juliet were simply lovers, and their names bring back to us no further thought than of their love and the lovely sorrow of its end; Antony are Cleopatra shall be before all things lovers, but the thought of their love and its triumphant tragedy shall recall other things beyond number—all the forces and all the fortunes of mankind, all the chance and all the consequence that waited on their imperial passion, all the infinite variety of qualities and powers wrought together and welded into the frame and composition of that love which shook from end to end all nations and kingdoms of the earth.

The same truth holds good in lighter matters; Biron and Rosaline in comedy are as simply lovers and no more as were their counterparts and coevals in tragedy: there is more in Benedick and Beatrice than this simple quality of love that clothes itself in the strife of wits; the injury done her cousin, which by the repercussion of its shock and refraction of its effect serves to transfigure with such adorable indignation and ardour of furious love and pity the whole bright light nature of Beatrice, serves likewise by a fresh reflection and counter-change of its consequence to exalt and enlarge the stature of her lover's spirit after a fashion beyond the reach of Shakespeare in his first stage. Mercutio again, like Philip, is a good friend and gallant swordsman, quick-witted and hot-blooded, of a fiery arid faithful temper, loyal and light and swift alike of speech and swordstroke; and this is all. But the character of the Bastard, clear and simple as broad sunlight though it be, has in it other features than this single and beautiful likeness of frank young manhood; his love of country and loathing of the Church that would bring it into subjection are two sides of the same national quality that has made and will always make every Englishman of his type such another as he was in belief and in unbelief, patriot and priest-hater; and no part of the design bears such witness to the full-grown perfection of his creator's power and skill as the touch that combines and fuses into absolute unity of concord the high and various elements of faith in England, loyalty to the wretched lord who has made him knight and acknowledged him kinsman, contempt for his abjection at the foul feet of the Church, abhorrence of his crime and constancy to his cause for something better worth the proof of war than his miserable sake who hardly can be roused, even by such exhortation as might put life and spirit into the dust of dead men's bones, to bid his betters stand and strike in defence of the country dishonoured by his reign.

It is this new element of variety in unity, this study of the complex and diverse shades in a single nature, which requires from any criticism worth attention some inquisition of character as complement to the investigation of style. Analysis of any sort would be inapplicable to the actors who bear their parts in the comic, the tragic or historic plays of the first period. There is nothing in them to analyse; they are, as we have seen, like all the characters represented by Marlowe, the embodiments or the exponents of single qualities and simple forces. The question of style also is therefore so far a simple question; but with the change and advance in thought and all matter of spiritual study and speculation this question also becomes complex, and inseparable, if we would pursue it to any good end, from the analysis of character and subject. In the debate on which we are now to enter, the question of style and the question of character, or as we might say the questions of matter and of spirit, are more than ever indivisible from each other, more inextricably inwoven than elsewhere into the one most difficult question of authorship which has ever been disputed in the dense and noisy school or fought out in the wide and windy field of Shakespearean controversy.

There can be few serious students of Shakespeare who have not sometimes felt that possibly the hardest problem involved in their study is that which requires for its solution some reasonable and acceptable theory as to the play of ***King Henry VIII.*** None such has ever yet been offered; and I certainly cannot pretend to supply one. Perhaps however it may be possible to do some service by an attempt to disprove what is untenable, even though it should not be possible to produce in its stead any positive proof of what we may receive as matter of absolute faith.

The veriest tiro in criticism who knows, anything of the subject in hand must perceive, what is certainly not beyond a schoolboy's range of vision, that the metre and the language of this play are in great part so like the language and the metre of Fletcher that the first and easiest inference would be to assume the partnership of that poet in the work. In former days it was Jonson whom the critics and commentators of their time saw good to select as the colleague or the editor of Shakespeare; but a later school of criticism has resigned the notion that the fifth act was retouched and adjusted by the author of *Volpone* to the taste of his patron James. The later theory is more plausible than this; the primary objection to it is that it is too facile and superficial. It is waste of time to point out with any intelligent and imaginative child with a tolerable ear for metre who had read a little of the one and the other poet could see for himself—that much of the play is externally as like the usual style of Fletcher as it is unlike the usual style of Shakespeare. The question is whether we can find one scene, one speech, one passage, which in spirit, in scope, in purpose, bears the same or any comparable resemblance to the work of Fletcher. I doubt if any man more warmly admires a poet whom few can have studied more thoroughly than I; and to whom, in spite of all sins of omission and commission,—and many and grievous they are, beyond the plenary absolution of even the most indulgent among critical confessors—I constantly return with a fresh sense of attraction, which is constantly rewarded by a fresh sense of gratitude and delight. It is assuredly from no wish to pluck a leaf from his laurel, which has no need of foreign grafts or stolen garlands from the loftier growth of Shakespeare's, that I venture to question his capacity for the work assigned to him by recent criticism. The speech of Buckingham, for example, on his way to execution, is of course at first sight very like the finest speeches of the kind in Fletcher; here is the same smooth and fluent declamation, the same prolonged and persistent melody, which if not monotonous is certainly not various; the same pure, lucid, perspicuous flow of simple rather than strong and elegant rather than exquisite English; and yet, if we set it against the best examples of the kind which may be selected from such tragedies as *Bonduca* or *The False One,* against the rebuke addressed by Caratach to his cousin or by Cæsar to the murderers of Pompey—and no finer instances of tragic declamation can be chosen from the work of this great master of rhetorical dignity and pathos—I cannot but think we shall perceive in it a comparative severity and elevation which will be missed when we turn back from it to the text of Fletcher. There is an aptness of phrase, an abstinence from excess, a "plentiful lack" of mere flowery and superfluous beauties, which we may rather wish than hope to find in the most famous of Shakespeare's successors. But if not his work, we may be sure it was his model; a model which he often approached, which he often studied, but which he never attained. It is never for absolute truth and fitness of expression, it is always for eloquence and sweetness, for fluency and fancy, that we find the tragic scenes of Fletcher most praiseworthy; and the motive or mainspring of interest is usually anything but natural or simple. Now the motive here is as simple the emotion as natural as possible; the author is content to dispense with all the violent or far-fetched or fantastic excitement from which Fletcher could hardly ever bring himself completely to abstain. I am not speaking here of those tragedies in which the hand of Beaumont is traceable; to these, I need hardly say, the charge is comparatively inapplicable which may fairly be brought against the unassisted works of his elder colleague; but in any of the typical tragedies of Fletcher, in *Thierry and* Theodoret, *in* Valentinian, *in* The Double Marriage, the scenes which for power and beauty of style may reasonably be compared with this of the execution of Buckingham will be found more forced in situation, more fanciful in language than this. Many will be found more beautiful, many more exciting; the famous interview of Thierry with the veiled Ordella, and the scene answering to this in the fifth act where Brunhalt is confronted with her dying son, will be at once remembered by all dramatic students; and the parts of Lucina and Juliana may each be described as a continuous arrangement of passionate and pathetic effects. But in which of these parts and in which of these plays shall we find a scene so simple, an effect so modest, a situation so unforced as here? where may we look for the same temperance of tone, the same control of excitement, the same steadiness of purpose? If indeed Fletcher could have written this scene, or the farewell of Wolsey to his greatness, or his parting scene with Cromwell, he was perhaps not a greater poet, but he certainly was a tragic writer capable of loftier self-control and severer self-command, than he has ever shown himself elsewhere.

And yet, if this were all, we might be content to believe that the dignity of the subject and the high example of his present associate had for once lifted the natural genius of Fletcher above itself. But the fine and subtle criticism of Mr. Spedding has in the main, I think, successfully and clearly indicated the lines of demarcation undeniably discernible in this play between the severer style of certain scenes or speeches and the laxer and more fluid style of others; between the graver, solider, more condensed parts of the apparently composite work, and those which are clearer, thinner, more diffused and diluted in expression. If under the latter head we had to class such passages only as the dying speech of Buckingham and the christening speech of Cranmer, it might after all be almost impossible to resist the internal evidence of Fletcher's handiwork. Certainly we hear the same soft continuous note of easy eloquence, level and limpid as a stream of crystalline transparence, in the plaintive adieu of the condemned statesman and the panegyrical prophecy of the favoured prelate. If this, I say, were all, we might admit that there is nothing—I have already admitted it—in either passage beyond the poetic reach of Fletcher. But on the hypothesis so ably maintained by the editor of Bacon there hangs no less a consequence than this: that we must assign to the same hand the crowning glory of the whole poem, the death-scene of Katherine. Now if Fletcher could have written that scene—a scene on which the only criticism ever passed, the only commendation ever bestowed, by the verdict of successive centuries, has been that of tears and-silence—if Fletcher could have written a scene so far beyond our applause, so far above our acclamation, then the memory of r o great poet has ever been so grossly wronged, so shamefully defrauded of its highest claim to honour. But, with all reverence for that memory, I must confess that I cannot bring myself to believe it. Any explanation appears to me more probable than this. Considering with what care every relic of his ·work was once and again collected by his posthumous editors—even to the attribution, not merely of plays in which he can have taken only the slightest part, but of plays in which we know that he had no share at all—I cannot believe that his friends would have let by far the brightest jewel in his crown rest unreclaimed in the then less popular treasure-house of Shakespeare. Belief or disbelief of this kind is however but a sandy soil for conjecture to build upon. Whether or not his friends would have reclaimed for him the credit of this scene, had they known it (as they must have known it) to be his due, I must repeat that such a miraculous example of a man's genius for once transcending itself and for ever eclipsing all its other achievements appears to me beyond all critical, beyond all theological credulity. Pathos and concentration are surely not among the dominant notes of Fletcher's style or the salient qualities of his intellect. Except perhaps in the beautiful and famous passage where Hengo dies in his uncle's arms, I doubt whether in any of the variously and highly coloured scenes played out upon the wide and shifting stage of his fancy the genius of Fletcher has ever unlocked the source of tears. Bellario and Aspatia were the children of his younger colleague; at least, after the death of Beaumont we meet no such figures on the stage of Fletcher. In effect, though Beaumont had a gift of grave sardonic humour which found especial vent in burlesques of the heroic style and in the systematic extravagance of such characters as Bessus, [Note 1: Compare with Beaumont's admirable farce of Bessus the Wretched imitation of it attempted after his death in the *Nice Valour* of Fletcher; whose proper genius was neither for pure tragedy nor broad farce, but for high comedy and heroic romance—a field of his own invention; witness *Monsieur Thomas* and *The Knight of Malta:* while Beaumont has approved himself in tragedy all but the worthiest disciple of Shakespeare, in farce beyond all comparison the aptest pupil of Jonson. He could give us no *Fox* or *Alchemist;* but the inventor of Bessus and Calianax was worthy of the esteem and affection returned to him by the creator of Morose and Rabbi Busy.] yet he was above all things a tragic poet; and though Fletcher had great power of tragic eloquence and passionate effusion yet his comic genius was of a rarer and more precious quality; one *Spanish Curate* is worth many a *Valentinian;* as, on the other hand, one *Philaster* is worth many a *Scornful Lady.* Now there is no question here of Beaumont; and there is no question that the passage here debated has been taken to the heart of the whole world and baptized in the tears of generations as no work of Fletcher's has ever been. That Beaumont could have written it I do not believe; but I am wellnigh assured that Fletcher could not I can scarcely imagine that the most fluid sympathy, the "hysteric passion" most easily distilled from the eyes of reader or spectator, can ever have watered with its tears the scene or the page which sets forth, however eloquently and effectively, the sorrows and heroisms of Ordella, Juliana, or Lucina. Every success but this I can well believe them, as they assuredly deserve, to have attained.

To this point then we have come, as to the crucial point at issue; and looking back upon those passages of the play which first suggest the handiwork of Fletcher, and which certainly do now and then seem almost identical in style with his, I think we shall hardly find the difference between these and other parts of the same play so wide and so distinct as the difference between the undoubted work of Fletcher and the undoubted work of Shakespeare. What that difference is we are fortunately able to determine with exceptional certitude, and with no supplementary help from conjecture of probabilities. In the play which is undoubtedly a joint work of these poets the points of contact and the points of disunion are unmistakable by the youngest eye. In the very last scene of *The Two Noble Kinsmen,* we can tell with absolute certainty what speeches were appended or interpolated by Fletcher; we can pronounce with positive conviction what passages were completed and what parts were left unfinished by Shakespeare. Even on Mr. Spedding's theory it can hardly be possible to do as much for *King Henry VIII.* The lines of demarcation, however visible or plausible, are fainter by far than these. It is certainly not much less strange to come upon such passages in the work of Shakespeare as the speeches of Buckingham and Cranmer than it would be to encounter in the work of Sophocles a sample of the later and laxer style of Euripides; to meet for instance in the *Antigone* with a passage which might pass muster as an extract from the *Iphigenia in Aulis.* In metrical effects the style of the lesser English poet is an exact counterpart of the style of the lesser Greek; there is the same comparative tenuity and fluidity of verse, the same excess of short unemphatic syllables, the same solution of the graver iambic into soft overflow of lighter and longer feet which relaxes and dilutes the solid harmony of tragic metre with notes of a more facile and feminine strain. But in *King Henry VIII.* it should be remarked that though we not unfrequently find the same preponderance as in Fletcher's work of verses with a double ending—which in English verse at least are not in themselves feminine, and need not be taken to constitute, as in Fletcher's case they do, a note of comparative effeminacy or relaxation in tragic style—we do not find the perpetual predominance of those triple terminations so peculiarly and notably dear to that poet; [Note 1: A desperate attempt was made to confute this argument by the production of a list in which such words as *slavery, emperor, pitying, difference,* and even *Christians,* were actually registered as trisyllabic terminations. To such unimaginable shifts are critics of the finger-counting or syllabic school inevitably and fatally reduced in the effort to establish by rule of thumb even so much as may seem verifiable by that rule in the province of poetical criticism. Prosody is at best no more than the skeleton of verse, as verse is the body of poetry; while the gain of such painful labourers in a field they know not how to till is not even a skeleton of worthless or irrelevant fact, but the shadow of such a skeleton reflected in water. It would seem that critics who hear only through their fingers have not even fingers to hear with.] so that even by the test of the metre-mongers who would reduce the whole question at issue to a point which might at once be solved by the simple process of numeration the argument in favour of Fletcher can hardly be proved tenable; for the metre which evidently has one leading quality in common with his is as evidently wanting in another at least as marked and as necessary to establish—if established it can be by any such test taken singly and apart from all other points of evidence—the collaboration of Fletcher with Shakespeare in this instance. And if the proof by mere metrical similitude is thus imperfect, there is here assuredly no other kind of test which may help to fortify the argument by any suggestion of weight even comparable to this. In those passages which would seem most plausibly to indicate the probable partnership of Fletcher, the unity and sustained force of the style keep it generally above the average level of his; there is less admixture or intrusion of lyric or elegiac quality; there is more of temperance and proportion alike in declamation and in debate. And throughout the whole play, and under all the diversity of composite subject and conflicting interest which disturbs the unity of action, there is a singleness of spirit, a general unity or concord of inner tone, in marked contrast to the utter discord and discrepancy of the several sections of *The Two Noble Kinsmen.* We admit, then, that this play offers us in some not unimportant passages the single instance of a style not elsewhere precisely or altogether traceable in Shakespeare; that no exact parallel to it can be found among his other plays; and that if not the partial work it may certainly be taken as the general model of Fletcher in his tragic poetry. On the other hand, we contend that its exceptional quality might perhaps be explicable as a tentative essay in a new line by one who tried so many styles before settling into his latest; and that, without far stronger, clearer, and completer proof than has yet been or can ever be advanced, the question is not solved but merely evaded by the assumption of a double authorship.

By far the ablest argument based upon a wider ground of reason or of likelihood than this of mere metre that has yet been advanced in support of the theory which would attribute a part of this play to some weaker hand than Shakespeare's is due to the study of a critic whose name—already by right of inheritance the most illustrious name of his age and ours—is now for ever attached to that of Shakespeare himself by right of the highest service ever done and the noblest duty ever paid to his memory. The untimely death which removed beyond reach of our thanks for all he had done and our hopes for all he might do the man who first had given to France the first among foreign poets—son of the greatest Frenchman and translator of the greatest Englishman—was only in this not untimely, that it forbore him till the great and wonderful work was done which has bound two deathless names together by a closer, than the common link that connects the names of all sovereign poets. Among all classic translations of the classic works of the world, I know of none that for absolute mastery and perfect triumph over all accumulation of obstacles, for supreme dominion over supreme difficulty, can be matched with the translation of Shakespeare by Francois-Victor Hugo; unless a claim of companionship may perchance be put in for Urquhart's unfinished version of Rabelais. For such success in the impossible as finally disproves the right of "that fool of a word" to existence—at least in the world of letters—the two miracles of study and of sympathy which have given Shakespeare to the French and Rabelais to the English, and each in his habit as he lived, may take rank together in glorious rivalry beyond eyeshot of all past or future competition.

Among the essays appended to the version of Shakespeare which they complete and illustrate, that which deals with the play now in question gives as ample proof as any other of the sound and subtle insight brought to bear by the translator upon the object of his labour and his love. His keen and studious intuition is here as always not less notable and admirable than his large and solid knowledge, his full and lucid comprehension at once of the text and of the history of Shakespeare's plays; and if his research into the inner details of that history may seem ever to have erred from the straight path of firm and simple certainty into some dubious byway of theory or conjecture, we may be sure at least that no lack of learning or devotion, of ardour or intelligence, but more probably some noble thought that was fathered by a noble wish to do honour to Shakespeare, has led him to attribute to his original some quality foreign to the text, or to question the authenticity of what for love of his author he might not wish to find in it. Thus he would reject the main part of the fifth act as the work of a mere court laureate, an official hack or hireling employed to anoint the memory of an archbishop and lubricate the steps of a throne with the common oil of dramatic adulation; and finding it in either case a task alike unworthy of Shakespeare to glorify the name of Cranmer or to deify the names of the queen then dead and the king yet living, it is but natural that he should be induced by an unconscious bias or prepossession of the will to depreciate the worth of the verse spent on work fitter for ushers and embalmers and the general valetry or varletry of Church and State. That this fifth act is unequal in point of interest to the better part of the preceding acts with which it is connected by so light and loose a tie of convenience is as indisputable as that the style of the last scene savours now and then, and for some space together, more strongly than ever of Fletcher's most especial and distinctive qualities, or that the whole structure of the play if judged by any strict rule of pure art is incomposite and incongruous, wanting in unity, consistency, and coherence of interest. The fact is that here even more than in *King John* the poet's hands were hampered by a difficulty inherent in the subject. To an English and Protestant audience, fresh from the passions and perils of reformation and reaction, he had to present an English king at war with the papacy, in whom the assertion of national independence was incarnate; and to the sympathies of such an audience it was a matter of mere necessity for him to commend the representative champion of their cause by all means which he could compel into the service of his aim. Yet this object was in both instances all but incompatible with the natural and necessary interest of the plot. It was inevitable that this interest should in the main be concentrated upon the victims of the personal or national policy of either king; upon Constance and Arthur, upon Katherine and Wolsey. Where these are not, either apparent in person on the stage, or felt in their influence upon the speech and action of the characters present, the pulse of the poem beats fainter and its forces begin to flag. In *King John* this difficulty was met and mastered, these double claims of the subject of the poem and the object of the poet were satisfied and harmonised by the effacement of John and the substitution of Faulconbridge as the champion of the national cause and the protagonist of the dramatic action. Considering this play in its double aspect of tragedy and history, we might say that the English hero becomes the central figure of the poem as seen from its historic side, while John remains the central figure of the poem as seen from its tragic side; the personal interest that depends on personal crime and retribution is concentrated on the agony of the king; the national interest which he, though the eponymous hero of the poem, was alike inadequate as a craven and improper as a villain to sustain and represent in the eyes of the spectators was happily and easily transferred to the one person of the play who could properly express within the compass of its closing act at once the protest against papal pretension, the defiance of foreign invasion, and the prophetic assurance of self-dependent life and self-sufficing strength inherent in the nation then fresh from a fiercer trial of its quality, which an audience of the days of Queen Elizabeth would justly expect from the poet who undertook to set before them in action the history of the days of King John. That history had lately been brought upon the stage under the hottest and most glaring light that could be thrown on it by the fire of fanatical partisanship; ***The Troublesome Reign of King John,*** weakest and most wooden of all wearisome chronicles that ever cumbered the boards, had in it for sole principle of life its power of congenial appeal to the same blatant and vulgar spirit of Protestantism which inspired it. In all the flat interminable morass of its tedious and tuneless verse I can find no blade or leaf of living poetic growth, no touch but one of nature or of pathos, where Arthur dying would fain send a last thought in search of his mother. From this play Shakespeare can have got neither hint nor help towards the execution of his own; the crude rough sketch of the Bastard as he brawls and swaggers through the long length of its scenes is hardly so much as the cast husk or chrysalid of the noble creature which was to arise and take shape for ever at the transfiguring touch of Shakespeare. In the case of ***King Henry VIII.*** he had not even such a blockish model as this to work from. The one preceding play known to me which deals professedly with the same subject treats of quite other matters than are handled by Shakespeare, and most notably with the scholastic adventures or misadventures of Edward Prince of Wales and his whipping-boy Ned Browne. A fresh and well-nigh a plausible argument might be raised by the critics who deny the unity of authorship in ***King Henry VIII.,*** on the ground that if Shakespeare had completed the work himself he would surely not have let slip the occasion to introduce one of the most famous and popular of all court fools in the person of Will Summers; who might have given life and relief to the action of many scenes now unvaried and unbroken in their gravity of emotion and event. Shakespeare, one would say, might naturally have been expected to take up and remodel the well-known figure of which his humble precursor could give but a rough thin outline, yet sufficient it should seem to attract the tastes to which it appealed; for this or some other quality of seasonable attraction served to float the now forgotten play of Samuel Rowley through several editions. The central figure of the huge hot-headed king, with his gusts of stormy good humour and peals of burly oaths which might have suited "Garagantua's mouth" and satisfied the requirements of Hotspur, appeals in a ruder fashion to the survival of the same sympathies on which Shakespeare with a finer instinct as evidently relied; the popular estimate of the bluff and brawny tyrant "who broke the bonds of Rome" was not yet that of later historians, though doubtless neither was it that of the writer or writers who would champion him to the utterance. Perhaps the opposite verdicts given by the instinct of the people on "bluff King Hal" and "Bloody Mary" may be understood by reference to a famous verse of Juvenal. The wretched queen was sparing of noble blood and lavish of poor men's lives—*cerdonibus timenda;* and the curses under which her memory was buried were spared by the people to her father, **Lamiarum cade madenti.** In any case, the humblest not less than the highest of the poets who wrote under the reign of his daughter found it safe to present him in a popular light before an audience of whose general prepossession in his favour William Shakespeare was no slower to take advantage than Samuel Rowley.

The two plays we have just discussed have one quality of style in common which has already been noted; that in them rhetoric is in excess of action or passion, and far in excess of poetry. They are not as yet perfect examples of his second manner, though far ahead of his first stage in performance as in promise. Compared with the full and living figure of Katherine or of Constance, the study of Margaret of Anjou is the mere sketch of a poet still in his pupilage: John and Henry, Faulconbridge and Wolsey, are designs beyond reach of the hand which drew the second and third Richard without much background or dramatic perspective. But the difficulties inherent in either subject are not surmounted throughout with absolute equality of success; the very point of appeal to the sympathy and excitement of the time may have been something of a disturbing force in the composition of the work—a loadstone rock indeed, of tempting attraction to the patriot as well as to the playwright, but possibly capable of proving in some measure a rock of offence to the poet whose ship was piloted towards it. His perfect triumph in the field of patriotic drama, coincident with the perfect maturity of his comic genius and his general style, has now to show itself.

    The great national trilogy which is at once the flower of Shakespeare's second period and the crown of his achievements in historic drama—unless indeed we so far depart from the established order and arrangement of his works as to include his three Roman plays in the same class with these English histories—offers perhaps the most singular example known to us of the variety in fortune which befell his works on their first appearance in print. None of these had better luck in that line at starting than ***King Henry IV.;*** none had worse than ***King Henry V.*** With ***Romeo and Juliet,*** the ***Merry Wives of Windsor,*** and ***Hamlet,*** it shares the remarkable and undesirable honour of having been seized and boarded by pirates even before it had left the dockyard. The master-builder's hands had not yet put the craft into seaworthy condition when she was overhauled by these Kidds and Blackbeards of the press. Of those four plays, the two tragedies at least were thoroughly recast, and rewritten from end to end: the pirated editions giving us a transcript, more or less perfect or imperfect, accurate or corrupt, of the text as it first came from the poet's hand; a text to be afterwards indefinitely modified and incalculably improved. Not quite so much can be said of the comedy, which certainly stood in less need of revision, and probably would not have borne it so well; nevertheless every little passing touch of the reviser's hand is here also a noticeable mark of invigoration and improvement But ***King Henry V.,*** we may fairly say, is hardly less than transformed. Not that it has been recast after the fashion of ***Hamlet,*** or even rewritten after the fashion of ***Romeo and Juliet;*** but the corruptions and imperfections of the pirated text are here more flagrant than in any other instance; while the general revision of style by which it is at once purified and fortified extends to every nook and corner of the restored and renovated building. Even had we, however, a perfect and trustworthy transcript of Shakespeare's original sketch for this play, there can be little doubt that the rough draught would still prove almost as different from the final masterpiece as is the soiled and ragged canvas now before us, on which we trace the outline of figures so strangely disfigured, made subject to such rude extremities of defacement and defeature. There is indeed less difference between the two editions in the comic than in the historic scenes; the pirates were probably more careful to furnish their market with a fair sample of the lighter than of the graver ware supplied by their plunder of the poet; Fluellen and Pistol lose less through their misusage than the king; and the king himself is less maltreated when he talks plain prose with his soldiers than when he chops blank verse with his enemies or his lords. His rough and ready courtship of the French princess is a good deal expanded as to length, but (if I dare say so) less improved and heightened in tone than we might well have wished and it might well have borne; in either text the hero's addresses savour rather of a ploughman than a prince, and his finest courtesies are clownish though not churlish. We may probably see in this rather a concession to the appetite of the groundlings than an evasion of the difficulties inherent in the subject-matter of the scene; too heavy as these might have been for another, we can conceive of none too hard for the magnetic tact and intuitive delicacy of Shakespeare's judgment and instinct. But it must fairly and honestly be admitted that in this scene we find as little of the charm and humour inseparable from the prince as of the courtesy and dignity to be expected from the king.

It should on the other hand be noted that the finest touch in the comic scenes, if not the finest in the whole portrait of Falstaff, is apparently an afterthought, a touch added on revision of the, original design. In the first scene of the second act Mrs. Quickly's remark that "he'll yield the crow a pudding one of these days" is common to both versions of the play; but the six words following are only to be found in the revised edition; and these six words the very pirates could hardly have passed over or struck out. They are not such as can drop from the text of a poet unperceived by the very dullest and horniest of human eyes. "The king has killed his heart" Here is the point in Falstaff's nature so strangely overlooked by the man of all men who we should have said must be the first to seize and to appreciate it. It is as grievous as it is inexplicable that the Shakespeare of France—the most infinite in compassion, in "conscience and tender heart," of all great poets in all ages and all nations of the world—should have missed the deep tenderness of this supreme and subtlest touch in the work of the greatest among his fellows. Again, with anything but "damnable" iteration, does Shakespeare revert to it before the close of this very scene. Even Pistol and Nym can see that what now ails their old master is no such ailment as in his prosperous days was but too liable to "play the rogue with his great toe." "The king hath run bad humours on the knight": "his heart is fracted, and corroborate." And it is not thus merely through the eclipse of that brief mirage, that fair prospect "of Africa, and golden joys," in view of which he was ready to "take any man's horses." This it is that distinguishes Falstaff from Panurge; that lifts him at least to the moral level of Sancho Panza. I cannot but be reluctant to set the verdict of my own judgment against that of Victor Hugo's; I need none to remind me what and who he is whose judgment I for once oppose, and what and who am I that I should oppose it; that he is he, and I am but myself; yet against his classification of Falstaff, against his definition of Shakespeare's unapproached and unapproachable masterpiece in the school of comic art and humoristic nature, I must and do with all my soul and strength protest. The admirable phrase of "swine-centaur" (*centaure du porc*) is as inapplicable to Falstaff as it is appropriate to Panurge. Not the third person but the first in date of that divine and human trinity of humourists whose names make radiant for ever the century of their new-born glory—not Shakespeare but Rabelais is responsible for the creation or the discovery of such a type as this. **"Suum cuique** is our Roman justice"; the gradation from Panurge to Falstaff is not downward but upward; though it be Victor Hugo's very self who asserts the contrary [Note 1: "La dynastie du bon sens, inaugurée dans Panurge, continuée dans Sancho Panca, tourne a mal et avorte dans Falstaff." (**William Shakespeare** deuxième partie, livre premier, ch. ii.)] Singular as may seem the collocation of the epithet "moral" with the name "Falstaff," I venture to maintain my thesis; that in point of feeling, and therefore of possible moral elevation, Falstaff is as undeniably the superior of Sancho as Sancho is unquestionably the superior of Panurge. The natural affection of Panurge is bounded by the self-same limits as the natural theology of Polyphemus; the love of the one, like the faith of the other, begins and ends alike at one point;

Myself,
And this great belly, first of deities;

(in which line, by the way, we may hear as it were a first faint prelude of the great proclamation to come—the hymn of praise and thanksgiving for the coronation day of King Gaster; whose laureate, we know, was as lovingly familiar with the Polyphemus of Euripides as Shakespeare with his own Pantagruel.) In Sancho we come upon a creature capable of love—but not of such love as kills or helps to kill, such love as may end or even as may seem to end in anything like heartbreak. "And now abideth Rabelais, Cervantes, Shakespeare, these three; but the greatest of these is Shakespeare."

I would fain score yet another point in the fat knight's favour; "I have much to say in the behalf of that Falstaff." Rabelais, evangelist and prophet of the Resurrection of the Flesh (so long entombed, ignored, repudiated, misconstrued, vilified, by so many generations and ages of Galilean preachers and Pharisaic schoolmen)—Rabelais was content to paint the flesh merely, in its honest human reality—human at least, if also bestial; in its frank and rude reaction against the half brainless and wholly bloodless teachers whose doctrine he himself on the one hand, and Luther on the other, arose together to smite severally—to smite them hip and thigh, even till the going down of the sun; the mock sun or marshy meteor that served only to deepen the darkness encompassing on every side the doubly dark ages—the ages of monarchy and theocracy, the ages of death and of faith. To Panurge, therefore, it was unnecessary and it might have seemed inconsequent to attribute other gifts or functions than are proper to such intelligence as may accompany the appetites of an animal. That most irreverend father in God, Friar John, belongs to a higher class in the moral order of being; and he much rather than his fellow-voyager and penitent is properly comparable with Falstaff. It is impossible to connect the notion of rebuke with the sins of Panurge. The actual lust and gluttony, the imaginary cowardice of Falstaff, have been gravely and sharply rebuked by critical morality; we have just noted a too recent and too eminent example of this; but what mortal ever dreamed of casting these qualities in the teeth of his supposed counterpart? The difference is as vast between Falstaff on the field of battle and Panurge on the storm-tossed deck as between Falstaff and Hotspur, Panurge and Friar John. No man could show cooler and steadier nerve than is displayed in either case—by the lay as well as the clerical namesake of the fourth evangelist. If ever fruitless but endless care was shown to prevent misunderstanding, it was shown in the pains taken by Shakespeare to obviate the misconstruction which would impute to Falstaff the quality of a Parolles or a Bobadil, a Bessus or a Moron. The delightful encounter between the jester and the bear in the crowning interlude of **La Princesse d'Elide** shows once more, I may remark, that Molière had sat at the feet of Rabelais as delightedly as Shakespeare before him. Such rapturous inebriety or Olympian incontinence of humour only fires the blood of the graver and less exuberant humourist when his lips are still warm and wet from the well-spring of the *Dive Bouteille.*

It is needless to do over again the work which was done, and well done, a hundred years since, by the writer whose able essay in vindication and exposition of the genuine character of Falstaff elicited from Dr. Johnson as good a jest and as bad a criticism as might have been expected. His argument is too thoroughly carried out at all points and fortified on all hands to require or even to admit of corroboration; and the attempt to appropriate any share of the lasting credit which is his due would be nothing less than a disingenuous impertinence. I may here however notice that in the very first scene of this trilogy which introduces us to the ever dear and honoured presence of Sir John, his creator has put into the mouth of a witness no friendlier or more candid than Ned Poins the distinction between two as true-bred cowards as ever turned back and one who will fight no longer than he sees reason. In this nutshell lies the whole kernel of the matter; the sweet, sound, ripe, toothsome, wholesome kernel of Falstaff's character and humour. He will fight as well as his princely patron, and, like the prince, as long as he sees reason; but neither Hal nor Jack has ever felt any touch of desire to pluck that "mere scutcheon" "honour "from the pale-faced moon." Harry Percy is as it were the true Sir Bedivere, the last of all Arthurian knights; Henry V. is the first as certainly as he is the noblest of those equally daring and calculating statesmen-warriors whose two most terrible, most perfect, and most famous types are Louis XI. and Cæsar Borgia. Gain, "commodity," the principle of self-interest which never but in word and in jest could become the principle of action with Faulconbridge,—himself already far more "a man of this world" than a Launcelot or a Hotspur,—is as evidently the mainspring of Henry's enterprise and life as of the contract between King Philip and King John. The I supple and shameless egotism of the churchmen on whose political sophistries he relies for external support is needed rather to varnish his project than to reassure his conscience. Like Frederic the Great before his first Silesian war, the future conqueror of

Agincourt has practically made up his mind before he seeks to find as good reason or as plausible excuse as were likewise to suffice the future conqueror of Rosbach. In a word, Henry is doubtless not the man, as old Auchindrane expresses it in the noble and strangely neglected tragedy which bears solitary but sufficient witness to the actual dramatic faculty of Sir Walter Scott's genius, to do the devil's work without his wages; but neither is he, on the like unprofitable terms, by any manner of means the man to do God's. No completer incarnation could be shown us of the militant Englishman—*Anglais pur sang;* but is not only, as some have seemed to think, with the highest, the purest, the noblest quality of English character that his just and far-seeing creator has endowed him. The godlike equity of Shakespeare's judgment, his implacable and impeccable righteousness of instinct and of insight, was too deeply ingrained in the very core of his genius to be perverted by any provincial or pseudo-patriotic prepossessions; his patriotism was too national to be provincial. Assuredly no poet ever had more than he: not even the king of men and poets who fought at Marathon and sang of Salamis: much less had any or has any one of our own, from Milton on to Campbell and from Campbell even to Tennyson. In the mightiest chorus of **King Henry V.** we hear the pealing ring of the same great English trumpet that was yet to sound over the battle of the Baltic, and again in our later day over a sea-fight of Shakespeare's own, more splendid and heart-cheering in its calamity than that other and all others in their triumph; a war-song and a sea-song divine and deep as death or as the sea, making thrice more glorious at once the glorious three names of England, of Grenville, and of Tennyson for ever. From the affectation of cosmopolitan indifference not Æschylus, not Pindar, not Dante's very self was more alien or more free than Shakespeare; but there was nothing of the dry Tyrtæan twang, the dull mechanic resonance as of wooden echoes from a platform, in the great historic chord of his lyre. "He is very English, too English, even," says the Master on whom his enemies alone—assuredly not his most loving, most reverent, and most thankful disciples—might possibly and plausibly retort that he was "very French, too French, even"; but he certainly was not "too English" to see and cleave to the main fact, the radical and central truth, of personal or national character, of typical history or tradition, without seeking to embellish, to degrade in either or in any way to falsify it. From king to king, from cardinal to cardinal, from the earliest in date of subject to the latest of his histories, we find the same thread running, the same link of honourable and righteous judgment, of equitable and careful equanimity, connecting and combining play with play in an unbroken and infrangible chain of evidence to the singleness of the poet's eye, the identity of the workman's hand, which could do justice and would do no more than justice, alike to Henry and to Wolsey, to Pandulph and to John. His typical English hero or historic protagonist is a man of their type who founded and built up the empire of England in India; a hero after the future pattern of Hastings and of Clive; not less daringly sagacious and not more delicately scrupulous, not less indomitable or more impeccable than they. A type by no means immaculate, a creature not at all too bright and good for English nature's daily food in times of mercantile or military enterprise; no whit more if no whit less excellent and radiant than reality. ***Amica Britannia, sed magis amica veritas.*** The master poet of England—all Englishmen may reasonably and honourably be proud of it—has not two weights and two measures for friend and foe. This palpable and patent fact, as his only and worthy French translator has well remarked, would of itself suffice to exonerate his memory from the imputation of having perpetrated in its evil entirety *The First Part of King Henry VI.*

There is, in my opinion, somewhat more of internal evidence than I have ever seen adduced in support of the tradition current from an early date as to the origin of the ***Merry Wives of Windsor;*** a tradition which assigns to Queen Elizabeth the same office of midwife with regard to this comedy as was discharged by Elwood with reference to ***Paradise Regained.*** Nothing could so naturally or satisfactorily explain its existence as the expression of a desire to see "Falstaff in love," which must have been nothing less than the equivalent of a command to produce him under the disguise of such a transfiguration on the boards, The task of presenting him so shorn of his beams, so much less than archangel (of comedy) ruined, and the excess of (humorous) glory obscured, would hardly, we cannot but think and feel, have spontaneously suggested itself to Shakespeare as a natural or eligible aim for the fresh exercise of his comic genius. To exhibit Falstaff as throughput the whole course of five acts a credulous and baffled dupe, one "easier to be played on than a pipe," was not really to reproduce him at all. The genuine Falstaff could no more have played such a part than the genuine Petruchio could have filled such an one as was assigned him by Fletcher in the luckless hour when that misguided poet undertook to continue the subject and to correct the moral of the next comedy in our catalogue of Shakespeare's. *The Tamer Tamed* is hardly less consistent or acceptable as a sequel to the *Taming of the Shrew* than the *Merry Wives of Windsor* as a supplement to *King Henry IV:* and no conceivable comparison could more forcibly convey how broad and deep is the gulf of incongruity which divides them.

The plea for once suggested by the author in the way of excuse or extenuation for this incompatibility of Falstaff with Falstaff—for the violation of character goes far beyond mere inconsistency or the natural ebb and flow of even the brightest wits and most vigorous intellects—will commend itself more readily to the moralist than to the humanist; in other words, to the preacher rather than to the thinker, the sophist rather than the artist. Here only does Shakespeare show that he feels the necessity of condescending to such evasion or such apology as is implied in the explanation of Falstaff's incredible credulity by a reference to "the guiltiness of his mind" and the admission, so gratifying to all minds more moral than his own, that "wit may be made a Jack-a-Lent, when 'tis upon ill employment." It is the best excuse that can be made; but can we imagine the genuine, the pristine Falstaff reduced to the proffer of such an excuse in serious good earnest?

In the original version of this comedy there was not a note of poetry from end to end; as it then appeared, it might be said to hold the same place on the roll of Shakespeare's plays as is occupied by *Bartholomew Fair* on the roll of Ben Jonson's. From this point of view it is curious to contrast the purely farcical masterpieces of the town-bred schoolboy and the country lad. There is a certain faint air of the fields, the river, and the park, even in the rough sketch of Shakespeare's farce—wholly prosaic as it is, and in no point suggestive of any unlikelihood in the report which represents it as the composition or rather as the improvisation of a fortnight. We know at once that he must have stroked the fallow greyhound that was outrun on "Cotsall"; that he must—and perhaps once or twice at least too often—have played truant (some readers, boys past or present, might wish for association's sake it could actually have been Datchet-wards) from under the shadow of good Sir Hugh's probably not over formidable though "threatening twigs of birch," at all risks of being "preeches" on his return, in fulfilment of the direful menace held out to that young namesake of his over whose innocence Mrs. Quickly was so creditably vigilant. On the other hand, no student of Jonson will need to be reminded how closely and precociously familiar the big stalwart Westminster boy, Camden's favoured and grateful pupil, must have made himself with the rankest haunts and most unsavoury recesses of that ribald waterside and Smithfield life which he lived to reproduce on the stage with a sometimes insufferable fidelity to details from which Hogarth might have shrunk. Even his unrivalled proficiency in classic learning can hardly have been the fruit of greater or more willing diligence in school hours than he must have lavished on other than scholastic studies in the streets. The humour of his huge photographic group of divers "humours" is undeniably and incomparably richer, broader, fuller of invention and variety, than any that Shakespeare's lighter work can show; all the five acts of the latter comedy can hardly serve as counterpoise, in weight arid wealth of comic effect, to the single scene in which Zeal-of-the-Land defines the moral and theological boundaries of action and intention which distinguish the innocent if not laudable desire to eat pig from the venial though not mortal sin of longing to eat pig in the thick of the profane Fair, which may rather be termed a foul than a fair. Taken from that point of view which looks only to force and freedom and range of humorous effect, Jonson's play is to his friend's as London is to Windsor; but in more senses than one it is to Shakespeare's as the Thames at London Bridge is to the Thames at Eton: the atmosphere of Smith-field is not more different from the atmosphere of the playing-fields; and some, too delicate of nose or squeamish of stomach, may prefer Cuckoo Weir to Shoreditch. But undoubtedly the phantoms of Shallow and Mrs. Quickly which put in (so to speak) a nominal reappearance in the **Merry Wives of Windsor** are comparatively as poor and thin if set over against the full rich outlines of Rabbi Busy and Dame Purecraft as these again are at all points alike inferior to the real Shallow and the genuine Quickly of **King Henry IV.** It is true that Jonson's humour has sometimes less in common with Shakespeare's than with the humour of Swift, Smollett, and Carlyle. For all his admiration and even imitation of Rabelais, Shakespeare has hardly once or twice burnt but so much as a stray pinch of fugitive incense on the altar of Cloacina; the only Venus acknowledged and adored by those three latter humourists. If not always constant with the constancy of Milton to the service of Urania, he never turns into a dirtier byway or back alley than the beaten path trodden occasionally by most of his kind which leads them on a passing errand of no unnatural devotion to the shrine of Venus Pandemos.

When, however, we turn from the raw rough sketch to the enriched and ennobled version of the present play we find it in this its better shape more properly comparable with another and a nobler work of Jonson's—with that magnificent comedy, the first avowed and included among his collection by its author, which according to all tradition first owed its appearance and success to the critical good sense and generous good offices of Shakespeare. Neither my duly unqualified love for the greater poet nor my duly qualified regard for the less can alter my sense that their mutual relations are in this one case inverted; that ***Every Man in his Humour*** is altogether a better comedy and a work, of higher art than the ***Merry Wives of Windsor.***

Kitely is to Ford almost what Arnolphe is to. Sganarelle. (As according to the learned Métaphraste "Filio non potest præferri nisi filius," even so can no one but Molière be preferred or likened to Molière.) Without actually touching like Arnolphe on the hidden springs of tragedy, the jealous husband in Jonson's play is only kept from trenching on the higher and forbidden grounds of passion by the potent will and the consummate self-command of the great master who called him up in perfect likeness to the life. Another or a deeper tone, another or a stronger touch, in the last two admirable scenes with his cashier and his wife, when his hot smouldering suspicion at length catches fire and breaks out in agony of anger, would have removed him altogether beyond the legitimate pale of comedy. As it is, the self-control of the artist is as thorough as his grasp and mastery of his subject are triumphant and complete.

It would seem as though on revision of the ***Merry Wives of Windsor*** Shakespeare had found himself unwilling or rather perhaps unable to leave a single work of his hand without one touch or breath on it of beauty or of poetry. The sole fitting element of harmonious relief or variety in such a case could of course be found only in an interlude of pure fancy; any touch of graver or deeper emotion would simply have untuned and deranged the whole scheme of composition. A lesser poet might have been powerless to resist the temptation or suggestion of sentiment that he should give to the little loves of Anne Page and Fenton a touch of pathetic or emotional interest; but "opulent as Shakespeare was, and of his opulence prodigal" (to borrow a phrase from Coleridge), he knew better than to patch with purple or embroider with seed-pearl the hem of this homespun little piece of comic drugget. The match between cloth of gold and cloth of frieze could hardly have borne any good issue in this instance. Instead therefore of following the lead of Terence's or the hint of Jonson's example, and exalting the accent of his comedy to the full-mouthed pitch of a Chremes or a Kitely, he strikes out some forty and odd lines of rather coarse and commonplace doggrel about brokers, proctors, lousy fox-eyed serjeants, blue and red noses, and so forth, to make room for the bright light interlude of fairyland child's-play which might not unfittingly have found place even within the moon-charmed circle of *A Midsummer Nights Dream.* Even in that all heavenly poem there are hardly to be found lines of more sweet and radiant simplicity than here.

The refined instinct, artistic judgment, and consummate taste of Shakespeare were perhaps never so wonderfully shown as in his recast of another man's work—a man of real if rough genius for comedy—which we get in the *Taming of the Shrew.* Only the collation of scene with scene, then of speech with speech, then of line with line, will show how much may be borrowed from a stranger's material and how much may be added to it by the same stroke of a single hand. All the force and humour alike of character and situation belong to Shakespeare's eclipsed and forlorn precursor; he has added nothing; he has tempered and enriched everything. That the luckless author of the first sketch is like to remain a man as nameless as the deed of the witches in *Macbeth,* unless some chance or caprice of accident should suddenly flash favouring light on his now impersonal and indiscoverable individuality, seems clear enough when we take into account the double and final disproof of his imaginary identity with Marlowe, which Mr. Dyce has put forward with such unanswerable certitude. He is a clumsy and coarse-fingered plagiarist from that poet, and his stolen jewels of expression look so grossly out of place in the homely setting of his usual style that they seem transmuted from real to sham. On the other hand, he is of all the Pre-Shakespeareans known to us incomparably the truest, the richest, the most powerful and original humourist; one indeed without a second on that ground, for "the rest are nowhere." Now Marlowe, it need scarcely be once again reiterated, was as certainly one of the least and worst among jesters as he was one of the best and greatest among poets. There can therefore be no serious question of his partnership in a play wherein the comic achievement is excellent and the poetic attempts are execrable throughout.

The recast of it in which a greater than Berni has deigned to play the part of that poet towards a lesser than Bojardo shows tact and delicacy perhaps without a parallel in literature. No chance of improvement is missed, while nothing of value is dropped or thrown away [Note 1: Possibly some readers may agree with my second thoughts, in thinking that one exception may here be made and some surprise be here expressed at Shakespeare's rejection of Sly's memorable query—"When will the fool come again, Sim?" It is true that he could well afford to spare it, as what could he not well afford to spare? but I will confess that it seems to me worthy of a place among his own Sly's most admirable and notable sallies of humour.] There is just now and then a momentary return perceptible to the skipping metre and fantastic manner of the first period, which may have been unconsciously suggested by the nature of the task in hand—a task of itself implying or suggesting some new study of old models; but the main style of the play in all its weightier parts is as distinctly proper to the second period, as clear an evidence of inner and spiritual affinity (with actual tabulation of dates, were such a thing as feasible as it is impossible, I must repeat that the argument would here be—what it is now—in no wise concerned), as is the handling of character throughout; but most especially the subtle force, the impeccable and careful instinct, the masculine delicacy of touch, by which the somewhat ruffianly temperament of the original Ferando is at once refined and invigorated through its transmutation into the hearty and humorous manliness of Petruchio's.

It is observable that those few and faint traces which we have noticed in this play of a faded archaic style trying as it were to resume a mockery of revirescence are not wholly even if mainly confined to the underplot which a suggestion or surmise of Mr. Collier's long since assigned to Haughton, author of ***Englishmen for my***

Money, or A Woman will have her Will: a spirited, vigorous, and remarkably regular comedy of intrigue, full of rough and ready incident, bright boisterous humour, honest lively provinciality and gay highhanded Philistinism. To take no account of this attribution would be to show myself as shamelessly as shamefully deficient in that respect and gratitude which all genuine and thankful students will always be as ready to offer as all thankless and insolent sciolists can ever be to disclaim, to the venerable scholar who since I was first engaged on these notes has added yet another obligation to the many under which he had already laid all younger and lesser labourers in the same field of study, by the issue in a form fitly ennobled and enriched of his great historical work on our early stage. It might seem something of an unintended impertinence to add that such recognition of his theory no more implies a blind acceptance of it—whatever such acceptance on my part might be worth—than the expression of such gratitude and respect could reasonably be supposed to imply an equally blind confidence in the authority or the value of that version of Shakespeare's text which has been the means of exposing a name so long and so justly honoured, not merely to the natural and rational inquisition of rival students, but to the rancorous and ribald obloquy of thankless and frontless pretenders.

Here perhaps as well as anywhere else I may find a proper place to intercalate the little word I have to say in partial redemption of my pledge to take in due time some notice at more or less length of the only two among the plays doubtfully ascribed to Shakespeare which in my eyes seem to bear any credible or conceivable traces of his touch. Of these two I must give the lesser amount of space and attention to that one which in itself is incomparably the more worthy of discussion, admiration, and regard. The reason of this lies in the very excellence which has attracted to it the notice of such competent judges and the suffrage of such eminent names as would make the task of elaborate commentary and analytic examination something more than superfluous on my part; whereas the other has never been and will never be assigned to Shakespeare by any critical student whose verdict is worth a minute's consideration or the marketable value of a straw. Nevertheless it is on other grounds worth notice; and such notice to be itself of any value, must of necessity be elaborate and minute. The critical analysis of **King Edward III** I have therefore relegated to its proper place in an appendix; while I reserve a corner of my text, at once out of admiration for the play itself and out of reverence for the names and authority of some who have given their verdict in its behalf, for a rough and rapid word or two on *Arden of Feversham.*

It is with equally inexpressible surprise that I find Mr. Collier accepting as Shakespeare's any part of *A Warning for Fair Women,* and rejecting without compromise or hesitation the belief or theory which would assign to the youth of Shakespeare the incomparably nobler tragic poem id question [Note 1: ***History of English Dramatic Poetry,*** ed. 1870, vol. ii. pp. 437-447. In a later part of his noble and invaluable work (vol. iii. p. 188) the author quotes a passage from "the induction to *A Warning for Fair Women,* 1599 (to which Shakespeare most assuredly contributed)." It will be seen that I do not shrink from admitting the full weight of authority which can be thrown into the scale against my own opinion. To such an assertion from the insolent organs of pretentious ignorance I should be content with the simple rejoinder that Shakespeare most assuredly did nothing whatever of the sort; but to return such an answer in the present case would be to write myself down—and that in company to which I should most emphatically object—as something very decidedly more—and worse—than an ass.] His first ascription to Shakespeare of *A Warning for Fair Women* is couched in terms far more dubious and diffident than such as he afterwards adopts. It "might," he says, "be given to Shakespeare on grounds far more plausible" (on what, except possibly those of date, I cannot imagine) "than those applicable to *Arden of Feversham*" He then proceeds to cite some detached lines and passages of undeniable beauty and vigour, containing equally undeniable coincidences of language, illustration, and expression with "passages in Shakespeare's undisputed plays." From these he passes on to indicate a "resemblance" which "is not merely verbal," and to extract whole speeches which "are Shakespearean in a much better sense"; adding in a surely too trenchant fashion, "Here we say, aut Shakespeare aut diabolus" I must confess, with all esteem for the critic and all admiration for the brief scene cited, that I cannot say, Shakespeare.

There are spirits of another sort from whom we naturally expect such assumptions and inferences as start from the vantage ground of a few separate or separable passages, and clear at a flying leap the empty space intervening which divides them from the goal of evidence as to authorship. Such a spirit was that of the late Mr. Simpson, to whose wealth of misused learning and fertility of misapplied conjecture I have already paid all due tribute; but who must have had beyond all other sane men—most assuredly, beyond all other fairly competent critics—the gift bestowed on him by a malignant fairy of mistaking assumption for argument and possibility for proof. He was the very Columbus of mare's nests; to the discovery of them, though they lay far beyond the pillars of Hercules, he would apply all shifts and all resources possible to an ultra-Baconian process of unphilosophical induction. On the devoted head of Shakespeare—who is also called Shakspere and Chaxpur—he would have piled a load of rubbish, among which the crude and vigorous old tragedy under discussion shines out like a veritable diamond of the desert. His "School of Shakspere," though not an academy to be often of necessity perambulated by the most peripatetic student of Shakespeare, will remain as a monument of critical or uncritical industry, a storehouse of curious if not of precious relics, and a warning for other than fair women—or fair scholars—to remember where "it is written that the shoemaker should meddle with his yard and the tailor with his last, the fisher with his pencil and the painter with his nets."

To me the difference appears immeasurable between the reasons for admitting the possibility of Shakespeare's authorship in the case of **Arden of Feversham,** and the pretexts for imagining the probability of his partnership in **A Warning for Fair Women.** There is a practically infinite distinction between the evidence suggested by verbal or even more than verbal resemblance of detached line to line or selected passage to passage, and the proof supplied by the general harmony and spiritual similarity of a whole poem, on comparison of it as a whole with the known works of the hypothetical author. This proof, at all events, we surely do not get from consideration in this light of the plea put forward in behalf of **A Warning for Fair Women.** This proof, I cannot but think, we are very much nearer getting from contemplation under the same light of the claim producible for **Arden of' Feversham.**

A Warning for Fair Women is unquestionably in its way a noticeable and valuable "piece of work," as Sly might have defined it. It is perhaps the best example anywhere extant of a merely realistic tragedy—of realism pure and simple applied to the service of the highest of the arts. Very rarely does it rise for a very brief interval to the height of tragic or poetic style, however simple and homely. The epilogue affixed to **Arden of Feversham** asks pardon of the "gentlemen" composing its audience for "this naked tragedy," on the plea that "simple truth is gracious enough" without needless ornament or bedizenment of "glozing stuff." Far more appropriate would such an apology have been as in this case was at least superfluous, if appended by way of epilogue to **A Warning for Fair Women.** That is indeed a naked tragedy; nine-tenths of it are in no wise beyond the reach of an able, industrious, and practised reporter, commissioned by the proprietors of the journal on whose staff he might be engaged to throw into the form of scenic dialogue his transcript of the evidence in a popular and exciting case of adultery and murder. The one figure on the stage of this author which stands out sharply defined in our recollection against a background of undistinguished shadows is the figure of the adulterer and murderer. This most discreditable of Browns has a distinct and brawny outline of his own, a gait and accent as of a genuine and recognisable man, who might have put to some better profit his shifty spirit of enterprise, his genuine capacity of affection, his burly ingenuity and hardihood. His minor confidants and accomplices, Mrs. Drury and her Trusty Roger, are mere common place profiles of malefactors: but it is in the contrast between the portraits of their two criminal heroines that the vast gulf of difference between the capacities of the two poets yawns patent to the sense of all readers. Anne Sanders and Alice Arden stand as far beyond comparison apart as might a portrait by any average academician and a portrait by Whistler or Legros. Once only, in the simple and noble scene cited by the over generous partiality of Mr. Collier, does the widow and murderess of Sanders rise to the tragic height of the situation and the dramatic level of the part so unfalteringly sustained from first to last by the wife and the murderess of Arden.

There is the self-same relative difference between the two subordinate groups of innocent or guilty characters. That is an excellent and effective touch of realism, where Brown comes across his victim's little boy playing truant in the street with a small schoolfellow; but in **Arden of Feversham** the number of touches as telling and as striking as this one is practically numberless. They also show a far stronger and keener faculty of poetic if not of dramatic imagination. The casual encounter of little Sanders with the yet red-handed murderer of his father is not comparable for depth and subtlety of effect with the scene in which Arden's friend Franklin, riding with him to Raynham Down, breaks off his "pretty tale" of a perjured wife, overpowered by a "fighting at his heart," at the moment when they come close upon the ambushed assassins in Alice Arden's pay. But the internal evidence in this case, as I have already intimated, does not hinge upon the proof or the suggestion offered by any single passage or by any number of single passages. The first and last evidence of real and demonstrable weight is the evidence of character. A good deal might be said on the score of style in favour of its attribution to a poet of the first order, writing at a time when there were but two such poets writing for the stage; but even this is here a point of merely secondary importance. It need only be noted in passing that if the problem be reduced to a question between the authorship of Shakespeare and the authorship of Marlowe there is no need and no room for further argument. The whole style of treatment from end to end is about as like the method of Marlowe as the method of Balzac is like the method of Dumas. There could be no alternative in that case; so that the actual alternative before us is simple enough: Either this play is the young Shakespeare's first tragic masterpiece, or there was a writer unknown to us then alive and at work for the stage who excelled him as a tragic dramatist not less—to say the very least—than he was excelled by Marlowe as a narrative and tragic poet

If we accept, as I have been told that Goethe accepted (a point which I regret my inability to verify), the former of these alternatives—or if at least we assume it for argument's sake in passing—we may easily strengthen our position by adducing as further evidence in its favour the author's thoroughly Shakespearean fidelity to the details of the prose narrative on which his tragedy is founded. But, it may be objected, we find the same fidelity to a similar text in the case of ***A Warning for Fair Women.*** And here again starts up the primal and radical difference between the two works: it starts up and will not be overlooked. Equal fidelity to the narrative text we do undoubtedly find in either case; the same fidelity we assuredly do not find. The one is a typical example of prosaic realism, the other of poetic reality.

A Study of Shakespeare

Light from darkness or truth from falsehood is not more infallibly discernible. The fidelity in the one case is exactly, as I have already indicated, the fidelity of a reporter to his notes. The fidelity in the other case is exactly the fidelity of Shakespeare in his Roman plays to the text of Plutarch. It is a fidelity which admits—I had almost written, which requires—the fullest play of the highest imagination. No more than the most realistic of reporters will it omit or falsify any necessary or even admissible detail; but the indefinable quality which it adds to the lowest as to the highest of these is (as Lamb says of passion) "the all in all in poetry." Turning again for illustration to one of the highest names in imaginative literature—a name sometimes most improperly and absurdly inscribed on the register of the realistic school, [Note 1: Not for the first and probably not for the last time I turn, with all confidence as with all reverence, for illustration and confirmation of my own words, to the exquisite critical genius of a long honoured and long lamented fellow-craftsman. The following admirable and final estimate of the more special element or peculiar quality in the intellectual force of Honoré de Balzac could only have been taken by the inevitable intuition and rendered by the subtlest eloquence of Charles Baudelaire. Nothing could more aptly and perfectly illustrate the distinction indicated in toy text between unimaginative realism and imaginative reality.

"I have many a time been astonished that to pass for an observer should be Balzac's great popular title to fame. To me it had always seemed that it was his chief merit to be a visionary, and a passionate visionary. All his characters are gifted with the ardour of life which animated himself. All his fictions are as deeply coloured as dreams. From the highest of the aristocracy to the lowest of the mob, all the actors in his ***Human Comedy*** are keener after living, more active and conning in their struggles, more staunch in endurance of misfortune, more ravenous in enjoyment, more angelic in devotion, than the comedy of the real world shows them to us. In a word, every one in Balzac, down to the very scullions, has genius. Every mind is a weapon loaded to the muzzle with will. It is actually Balzac himself. And as all the beings of the outer world presented themselves to his mind's eye in strong relief and with a telling expression, he has given a convulsive action to his figures; he has blackened their shadows and intensified their lights. Besides, his prodigious love of detail, the outcome of an immoderate ambition to see everything, to bring everything to sight, to guess everything, to make others guess everything, obliged him to set down more forcibly the principal lines, so as to preserve the perspective of the whole. He reminds me sometimes of those etchers who are never satisfied with the biting-in of their outlines, and transform into very ravines the main scratches of the plate. From this astonishing natural disposition of mind wonderful results have been produced. But this disposition is generally defined as Balzac's great fault. More properly speaking, it is exactly his great distinctive quality. But who can boast of being so happily gifted, and of being able to apply a method which may permit him to invest—and that with a sure hand—what is purely trivial with splendour and imperial purple? Who can do this? Now, he who does not, to speak the truth, does no great thing."

Nor was any very great thing done by the author of *A Warning for Fair Women.*] we may say that the difference on this point is not the difference between Balzac and Dumas, but the distinction between Balzac and M. Zola. Let us take by way of example the character next in importance to that of the heroine—the character of her paramour. A viler figure was never sketched by Balzac; a viler figure was seldom drawn by Thackeray. But as with Balzac, so with the author of this play, the masterful will combining with the masterly art of the creator who fashions out of the worst kind of human clay the breathing likeness of a creature so hatefully pitiful and so pitifully hateful overcomes, absorbs, annihilates all sense of such abhorrence and repulsion as would prove the work which excited them no high or even true work of art. Even the wonderful touch of dastardly brutality and pitiful self-pity with which Mosbie at once receives and repels the condolence of his mistress on his wound—

Alice.—Sweet Mosbie, hide thine arm, it kills my heart.
Mosbie,—Ay, Mistress Arden, this is your favour.—

even this does not make unendurable the scenic representation of what in actual life would be unendurable for any man to witness. Such an exhibition of currish cowardice and sullen bullying spite increases rather our wondering pity for its victim than our wondering sense of her degradation, And this is a kind of triumph which only such an artist as Shakespeare in poetry or as Balzac in prose can achieve.

Alice Arden, if she be indeed a daughter of Shakespeare's, is the eldest born of that group to which Lady Macbeth and Dionyza belong by right of weird sisterhood. The wives of the thane of Glamis and the governor of Tharsus, it need hardly be said, are both of them creations of a much later date—if not of the very latest discernible or definable stage in the art of Shakespeare. Deeply dyed as she is in bloodguiltiness, the wife of Arden is much less of a born criminal than these. TO her, at once the agent and the patient of her crime, the victim and the instrument of sacrifice and blood-offering to Venus Libitina, goddess of love and death,—to her, even in the deepest pit of her deliberate wickedness, remorse is natural and redemption conceivable. Like the Phaedra of Racine, and herein so nobly unlike the Phædra of Euripides, she is capable of the deepest and bitterest penitence,—incapable of dying with a hideous and homicidal falsehood on her long polluted lips. Her latest breath is not a lie but a prayer.

Considering, then, in conclusion, the various and marvellous gifts displayed for the first time on our stage by the great poet, the great dramatist, the strong and subtle searcher of hearts, the just and merciful judge and painter of human passions, who gave this tragedy to the new-born literature of our drama; taking into account the really wonderful skill, the absoluteness of intuition and inspiration, with which every stroke is put in that touches off character or tones down effect, even in the sketching and grouping of such minor figures as the ruffianly hireling Black Will, the passionate artist without pity or conscience, [Note 1: I do not know or remember in the whole radiant range of Elizabethan drama more than one parallel tribute to that paid in this play by an English poet to the yet foreign art of painting, through the eloquent mouth of this enthusiastic villain of genius, whom we might regard as a more genuinely Titianic sort of Wainwright. The parallel passage is that most lovely and fervid of all imaginative panegyrics on this art, extracted by Lamb from the comedy of **Doctor Dodipoll;** which saw the light or twilight of publication just eight years later than **Arden of Feversham.**] and above all the "unimitated, inimitable" study of Michael, in whom even physical fear becomes tragic, and cowardice itself no ludicrous infirmity but rather a terrible passion; I cannot but finally take heart to say, even in the absence of all external or traditional testimony, that it seems to me not pardonable merely nor permissible, but simply logical and reasonable, to set down this poem, a young man's work on the face of it, as the possible work of no man's youthful hand but Shakespeare's.

No similar question is raised, no parallel problem stated, in the case of any one other among the plays now or ever ascribed on grounds more or less dubious to that same indubitable hand. This hand I do not recognise even in the ***Yorkshire Tragedy,*** full as it is to overflowing of fierce animal power, and hot as with the furious breath of some caged wild beast. Heywood, who as the most realistic and in some sense prosaic dramatist of his time has been credited (though but in a modestly tentative and suggestive fashion) with its authorship, was as incapable of writing it as Chapman of writing the Shakespearean parts of ***The Two Noble Kinsmen*** or Fletcher of writing the scenes of Wolsey's fall and Katherine's death in ***King Henry VIII*** To the only editor of Shakespeare responsible for the two earlier of the three suggestions here set aside, they may be forgiven on the score of insufficient scholarship and want of critical training; but on what ground the third suggestion can be excused in the case of men who should have a better right than most others to speak with some show of authority on a point of higher criticism, I must confess myself utterly at a loss to imagine. In the ***Yorkshire Tragedy*** the submissive devotion of its miserable heroine to her maddened husband is merely doglike,—though not even, in the exquisitely true and tender phrase of our sovereign poetess, 'most passionately patient." There is no likeness in this poor trampled figure to "one of Shakespeare's women": Griselda was no ideal of his. To find its parallel in the dramatic literature of the great age, we must look to lesser great men than Shakespeare. Ben Jonson, a too exclusively masculine poet, will give us a couple of companion figures for her—or one such figure at least; for the wife of Fitzdottrel, submissive as she is even to the verge of undignified if not indecorous absurdity, is less of a human spaniel than the wife of Corvino. Another such is Robert Davenport's Abstemia, so warmly admired by Washington Irving; another is the heroine of that singularly powerful and humorous tragicomedy, labelled ***How to Choose a Good Wife from a Bad,*** which in its central situation anticipates that of Leigh Hunt's beloved and lovely ***Legend*** *of Florence;* while Decker has revived, in one of our sweetest and most graceful examples of dramatic romance, the original incarnation of that somewhat pitiful ideal which even in a ruder and more Russian century of painful European progress out of night and winter could only be made credible, acceptable, or endurable, by the yet unequalled genius of Chaucer and Boccaccio.

For concentrated might and overwhelming weight of realism, this lurid little play beats ***A Warning for Fair Women*** fairly out of the field. It is and must always be (I had nearly said, thank. heaven) unsurpassable for pure potency of horror; and the breathless heat of the action, its raging rate of speed, leaves actually no breathing-time for disgust; it consumes our very sense of repulsion as with fire. But such power as this, though a rare and a great gift, is not the right quality for a dramatist; it is not the fit property of a poet Ford and Webster, even Tourneur and Marston, who have all been more or less wrongfully though more or less plausibly attacked on the score of excess in horror, have none of them left us anything so nakedly terrible, so terribly naked as this. Passion is here not merely stripped to the skin but stripped to the bones. I cannot tell who could and I cannot guess who would have written it. " 'Tis a very excellent piece of work"; may we never exactly look upon its like again!

I thought it at one time far from impossible, if not very nearly probable, that the author of ***Arden of Feversham*** might be one with the author of the famous additional scenes to ***The Spanish Tragedy,*** and that either both of these "pieces of work" or neither must be Shakespeare's. I still adhere to Coleridge's verdict, which indeed must be that of all judges capable of passing any sentence worthier of record than are

Fancies too weak for boys, too green and idle
For girls of nine:

to the effect that those magnificent passages, well-nigh overcharged at every point with passion and subtlety, sincerity and instinct of pathetic truth, are no less like Shakespeare's work than unlike Jonson's: thoughhardly perhaps more unlike the typical manner of his adult and matured style than is the general tone of ***The***

Case is Altered, his one surviving comedy of that earlier period in which we know from Henslowe that the stout-hearted and long struggling young playwright went through so much theatrical hackwork and piecework in the same rough harness with other now more or less notable workmen then drudging under the manager's dull narrow sidelong eye for bare bread and bare: shelter. But this unlikeness, great as it is and serious and singular, between his former and his latter style in high comedy, gives no warrant for us to believe him capable of so immeasurable a transformation in tragic style and so indescribable a decadence in tragic power as would be implied in a descent from the "fine madness" of "old Jeronymo" to the flat sanity and smoke-dried sobriety of ***Catiline*** and ***Sejanus.***—I cannot but think, too that Lamb's first hypothetical ascription of these wonderful scenes to Webster, so much the most Shakespearean in gait and port and accent of all Shakespeare's liege men-at-arms, was due to a far happier and more trustworthy instinct than led him in later years to liken them rather to "the overflowing griefs and talking distraction of Titus Andronicus."

We have wandered it may be somewhat out of the right time into a far other province of poetry than the golden land of Shakespeare's ripest harvest-fields of humour. And now, before we may enter the "flowery square" made by the summer growth of his four greatest works in pure and perfect comedy "beneath a broad and equal blowing wind" of all happiest and most fragrant imagination, we have but one field to cross, one brook to ford, that hardly can be thought to keep us out of Paradise. In the garden-plot on whose wicket is inscribed ***All's Well that Ends Well,*** we are hardly distant from Eden itself

About a young dove's flutter from a wood.

The ninth story of the third day of the Decameron is one of the few subjects chosen by Shakespeare—as so many were taken by Fletcher—which are less fit, we may venture to think, for dramatic than for narrative treatment. He has here again shown all possible delicacy of instinct in handling a matter which unluckily it was not possible to handle on the stage with absolute and positive delicacy of feeling or expression. Dr. Johnson—in my humble opinion, with some justice; though his verdict has been disputed on the score of undeserved austerity—"could not reconcile his heart to Bertram"; and I, unworthy as I may be to second or support on the score of morality the finding of so great a moralist, cannot reconcile my instincts to Helena. Parolles is even better than Bobadil, as Bobadil is even better than Bessus; and Lafeu is one of the very best old men in all the range of comic art. But the whole charm and beauty of the play, the quality which raises it to the rank of its fellows by making it loveable as well as admirable, we find only in the "sweet serene, skylike" sanctity and attraction of adorable old age, made more than ever near and dear to us in the incomparable figure of the old Countess of Roussillon. At the close of the play, Fletcher would inevitably have married her to Lafeu—or rather possibly, to the King.

At the entrance of the heavenly quadrilateral, or under the rising dawn of the four fixed stars which compose our Northern Cross among the constellations of dramatic romance hung high in the highest air of poetry, we may well pause for very dread of our own delight, lest unawares we break into mere babble of childish rapture and infantile thanksgiving for such light vouchsafed even to our "settentrional vedovo sito" that even at their first dawn out of the depths

Goder pareva il ciel di lor fiammelle.

Beyond these again we see a second group arising, the supreme starry trinity of the ***Winter's Tale,*** the ***Tempest,*** and ***Cymbeline:*** and beyond these the divine darkness of everlasting and all-maternal night These seven lamps of the romantic drama have in them—if I may strain the similitude a little further yet—more of lyric light than could fitly be lent to feed the fire or the sunshine of the worlds of pure tragedy or comedy. There is more play, more vibration as it were, in the splendours of their spheres. Only in the heaven of Shakespeare's making can we pass and repass at pleasure from he sunny to the stormy lights, from the glory of ***Cymbeline*** to the glory of ***Othello.***

In this first group of four—wholly differing on that point from the later constellation of three—there is but very seldom, not more than once or twice at most, a shooting or passing gleam of anything more lurid or less lovely than "a light of laughing flowers." There is but just enough of evil or even of passion admitted into their sweet spheres of life to proclaim them living: and all that does find entrance is so tempered by the radiance of the rest that we retain but softened and lightened recollections even of Shylock and Don John when we think of the **Merchant of Venice** and **Much Ado about Nothing;** we hardly feel in **As You Like It** the presence or the existence of Oliver and Duke Frederick; and in **Twelfth Night,** for all its name of the midwinter, we find nothing to remember that might jar with the loveliness of love and the summer light of life.

No astronomer can ever tell which if any one among these four may be to the others as a sun; for in this special tract of heaven "one star differeth" not "from another star in glory." From each and all of them, even "while this muddy vesture of decay doth grossly close [us] in," we cannot *but* hear the harmony of a single immortal soul

Still quiring to the young-eyed cherubins.

The coincidence of the divine passage in which I have for once permitted myself the freedom of altering for quotation's sake one little word, with a noble excerpt given by Hallam from the Latin prose writings of Campanella, may recall to us with a doubly appropriate sense of harmonious fitness the subtly beautiful image of Mr. Tennyson;—

Star to star vibrates light: may soul to soul
Strike thro' a finer element of her own?

Surely, if ever she may, such a flash might we fancy to have passed from the spirit of the most glorious martyr and poet to the spirit of the most glorious poet and artist upon the face of the earth together. Even to Shakespeare any association of his name with Campanella's, as even to Campanella any association of his name with Shakespeare's, cannot but be an additional ray of honour: and how high is the claim of the divine philosopher to share with the godlike dramatist their common and crowning name of poet, all Englishmen at least may now perceive by study of Campanella's sonnets in the noble and exquisite version of Mr. Symonds; to whom among other kindred debts we owe no higher obligation than is due to him as the giver of these poems to the inmost heart of all among his countrymen whose hearts are worthy to hold and to hoard up such treasure.

Where nothing at once new and true can be said, it is always best to say nothing; as it is in this case to refrain from all reiteration of rhapsody which must have been somewhat "mouldy ere" any living man's "grandsires had nails on their toes," if not at that yet remoter date "when King Pepin of France was a little boy" and "Queen Guinever of Britain was a little wench." In the ***Merchant of Venice,*** at all events, there is hardly a single character from Portia to old Gobbo, a single incident from the exaction of Shylock's bond to the computation of hairs in Launcelot's beard and Dobbin's tail, which has not been more plentifully beprosed than ever Rosalind was berhymed. Much wordy wind has also been wasted on comparison of Shakespeare's Jew with Marlowe's; that is, of a living subject for terror and pity with a mere mouthpiece for the utterance of poetry as magnificent as any but the best of Shakespeare's.

Nor can it well be worth any man's while to say or to hear for the thousandth time that ***As You Like It*** would be one of those works which prove, as Landor said long since, the falsehood of the stale axiom that no work of man's can be perfect, were it not for that one unlucky slip of the brush which has left so ugly a little smear in one corner of the canvas as the betrothal of Oliver to Celia; though, with all reverence for a great name and a noble memory, I can hardly think that matters were much mended in George Sand's adaptation of the play by the transference of her hand to Jaques. Once elsewhere, or twice only at the most, is any such other sacrifice of moral beauty or spiritual harmony to the necessities and traditions of the stage discernible in all the world-wide work of Shakespeare. In the one case it is unhappily undeniable; no man's conscience, no conceivable sense of right and wrong, but must more or less feel as did Coleridge's the double violence done it in the upshot of ***Measure for Measure.*** Even in the much more nearly spotless work which we have next to glance at, some readers have perhaps not unreasonably found a similar objection to the final good fortune of such a pitiful fellow as Count Claudio. It will be observed that in each case the sacrifice is made to comedy. The actual or hypothetical necessity of pairing off all the couples after such a fashion as to secure a nominally happy and undeniably matrimonial ending is the theatrical idol whose tyranny exacts this holocaust of higher and better feelings than the mere liquorish desire to leave the board of fancy with a palatable morsel of cheap sugar on the tongue.

If it is proverbially impossible to determine by selection the greatest work of Shakespeare, it is easy enough to decide on the date and the name of his most perfect comic masterpiece. For absolute power of composition, for faultless balance and blameless rectitude of design, there is unquestionably no creation of his hand that will bear comparison with **_Much Ado About Nothing._** The ultimate marriage of Hero and Claudio, on which I have already remarked as in itself a doubtfully desirable consummation, makes no flaw in the dramatic perfection of a piece which could not otherwise have been wound up at all. This was its one inevitable conclusion, if the action were not to come to a tragic end; and a tragic end would here have been as painfully and as grossly out of place as is any but a tragic end to the action of **_Measure for Measure._** As for Beatrice, she is as perfect a lady, though of a far different age and breeding, as Célimène or Millamant; and a decidedly more perfect woman than could properly or permissibly have trod the stage of Congreve or Molière. She would have disarranged all the dramatic proprieties and harmonies of the one great school of pure comedy. The good fierce outbreak of her high true heart in two swift words—"Kill Claudio" [Note 1: I remember to have somewhere at some time fallen in with some remark by some commentator to some such effect as this: that it would be somewhat difficult to excuse the unwomanly violence of this demand. Doubtless it would. And doubtless it would be somewhat more than difficult to extenuate the unmaidenly indelicacy of Jeanne Darc.]—would have fluttered the dovecotes of fashionable drama to some purpose. But Alceste would have taken her to his own.

No quainter and apter example was ever given of many men's absolute inability to see the plainest aims, to learn the simplest rudiments, to appreciate the most practical requisites of art, whether applied to theatrical action or to any other as evident as exalted aim, than the instance afforded by that criticism of time past which sagaciously remarked that "any less amusingly absurd" constables than Dogberry and Verges would have filled their parts in the action of the play equally well. Our own day has doubtless brought forth critics and students of else unparalleled capacity for the task of laying wind-eggs in mare's nests, and wasting all the warmth of their brains and tongues in the hopeful endeavour to hatch them: but so fine a specimen was never dropped yet as this of the plumed or plumeless biped who discovered that if Dogberry had not been Dogberry and Verges had not been Verges they would have been equally unsuccessful in their honest attempt to warn Leonato betimes of the plot against his daughter's honour. The only explanation of the mistake is this; and it is one of which the force will be intelligible only to those who are acquainted with the very singular physiology of that remarkably prolific animal known to critical science as the Shakespearean scholiast: that if Dogberry had been other than Dogberry, or if Verges had been other than Verges, the action and catastrophe of the whole play could never have taken place at all.

All true Pantagruelians will always, or at least as long as may be permitted by the Society for the Suppression of Vice, cherish with an especial regard the comedy in which Shakespeare also has shown himself as surely the loving as he would surely have been the beloved disciple of that insuppressible divine, the immortal and most reverend vicar of Meudon. Two only among the mighty men who lived and wrote and died within the century which gave birth to Shakespeare were found worthy of so great an honour at his hands as the double homage of citation and imitation; and these two, naturally and properly enough, were François Rabelais and Christopher Marlowe. We cannot but recognise on what far travels in what good company "Feste the jester" had but lately been, on that night of "very gracious fooling" when he was pleased to enlighten the unforgetful mind of Sir Andrew as to the history of Pigrogromitus, and of the Vapians passing the equinoctial of Queubus. At what precise degree of latitude and longitude between the blessed islands of Medamothy and Papimania this equinoctial may intersect the Sporades of the outer ocean, is a problem on the solution of which the energy of those many modern sons of Aguecheek who have undertaken the task of writing about and about the text and the history of Shakespeare might be expended with an unusually reasonable hope and expectation of arriving at an exceptionally profitable end.

Even apart from their sunny identity of spirit and bright sweet brotherhood of style, the two comedies of ***Twelfth Night*** and ***As You Like It*** would stand forth confessed as the common offspring of the same spiritual period by force and by right of the trace or badge they proudly and professedly bear in common, as of a recent touch from the ripe and rich and radiant influence of Rabelais. No better and no fuller vindication of his happy memory could be afforded than by the evident fact that the two comedies which bear the imprint of his sign-manual are among all Shakespeare's works as signally remarkable for the cleanliness as for the richness of their humour. Here is the right royal seal of Pantagruel, clean-cut and clearly stamped, and unincrusted with any flake of dirt from the dubious finger of Panurge. In the comic parts of those plays in which the humour is rank and flagrant that exhales from the lips of Lucio, of Boult, or of Thersites, there is no trace or glimpse of Rabelais. From him Shakespeare has learnt nothing and borrowed nothing that was not wise and good and sweet and clean and pure. All the more honour, undoubtedly, to Shakespeare, that he would borrow nothing else: but assuredly, also, all the more honour to Rabelais, that he had enough of this to lend.

It is less creditable to England than honourable to France that a Frenchman should have been the first of Shakespearean students to discover and to prove that the great triad of his Roman plays is not a consecutive work of the same epoch. Until the appearance of François-Victor Hugo's incomparable translation, with its elaborate and admirable commentary, it seems to have been the universal and certainly a most natural habit of English criticism to take the three as they usually appear together, in the order of historical chronology, and by tacit implication to assume that they were composed in such order. I should take some shame to myself but that I feel more of grateful pride than of. natural shame in the avowal that I at all events owe the first revelation of the truth now so clear and apparent in this matter, to the son of the common lord and master of all poets born in his age—be they liege subjects as loyal as myself or as contumacious as I grieve to find one at least of my elders and betters, whenever I perceive—as too often I cannot choose but perceive—that the voice is the voice of Arnold, but the hand is the hand of Sainte-Beuve

To the honoured and lamented son of our beloved and glorious Master, whom neither I nor any better man can ever praise and thank and glorify enough, belongs all the credit of discerning for himself and discovering for us all the truth that Julius Cæsar *is at all points equally like the greatest works of Shakespeare's middle period and unlike the works of his last. It is in the main a play belonging to the same order as* King Henry IV.; but it differs from our English Henriade—as remarkably unlike Voltaire's as Zaïre *is unlike* Othello—not more by the absence of Falstaff than by the presence of Brutus. Here at least Shakespeare has made full amends, if not to all modern democrats, yet assuredly to all historical republicans, for any possible or apparent preference of royal to popular traditions. Whatever manner of man may have been the actual Roman, our Shakespearean Brutus is undoubtedly the very noblest figure of a typical and ideal republican in all the literature of the world. "A democracy such as yours in America is my abhorrence," wrote Landor once to an impudent and foul-mouthed Yankee philosophaster (this word, permissible or not, but certainly convenient, is none of mine, but belongs to the late Mr. Kingsley), who had intruded himself on that great man's privacy in order to have the privilege of afterwards informing the readers of a pitiful pamphlet on England that Landor had "pestered him with Southey"; an impertinence, I may add, which Mr. Landor at once rebuked with the sharpest contempt and chastised with the haughtiest courtesy. But, the old friend and lifelong champion of Kossuth went on to say, his feelings were far different towards a republic; and if on the one point, then not less certainly on the other, we may be assured that his convictions and his prepossessions would have been shared by the author of *Coriolanus* and Julius Cæsar.

Having now come perforce to the inevitable verge of *Hamlet,* I hasten to declare that I can advance no pretension to compete with the claim of that "literary man" who became immortal by dint of one dinner with a bishop, and in right of that last glass poured out for him in sign of amity by "Sylvester Blougram, styled *in partibus Episcopus, necnon* the deuce knows what." I do not propose to prove my perception of any point in the character of Hamlet "unseized by the Germans yet." I can only determine, as the Church Catechism was long since wont to bid me, "to keep my hands from picking and stealing, and my tongue" not only" from evil-speaking, lying, and slandering"—though this itself is a form of abstinence not universally or even commonly practised among the rampant rout of rival commentators—but also, now as ever throughout this study, from all conscious repetition of what others have said before me.

In ***Hamlet,*** as it seems to me, we set foot as it were on the bridge between the middle and the final period of Shakespeare. That priceless waif of piratical salvage which we owe to the happy rapacity of a hungry publisher is of course more accurately definable as the first play of ***Hamlet*** than as the first edition of the play. And this, first ***Hamlet,*** on the whole, belongs altogether to the middle period. The deeper complexities of the subject are merely indicated. Simple and trenchant outlines of character are yet to be supplanted by features of subtler suggestion and infinite interfusion. Hamlet himself is almost more of a satirist than a philosopher: Asper and Macilente, Felice and Malevole, the grim studies after Hamlet unconsciously or consciously taken by Jonson and Marston, may pass as wellnigh passable imitations, with an inevitable streak of caricature in them, of the first Hamlet; they would have been at once puerile and ghastly travesties of the second. The Queen, whose finished figure is now something of a riddle, stands out simply enough in the first sketch as confidant of Horatio if not as accomplice of Hamlet. There is not more difference between the sweet quiet flow of those plain verses which open the original play within the play and the stiff sonorous tramp of their substitutes, full-charged with heavy classic artillery of Phœbus and Neptune and Tellus and Hymen, than there is btween the straightforward agents of their own destiny whom we meet in the fist ***Hamlet*** and the obliquely moving patients who veer sideways to their doom in the second.

This minor transformation of style in the inner play, made solely with the evident view of marking the distinction between its duly artificial forms of speech and the duly natural forms of speech passing between the spectators, is but one among innumerable indications which only a purblind perversity of prepossession can overlook of the especial store set by Shakespeare himself on this favourite work, and the exceptional pains taken by him to preserve it for aftertime in such fullness of finished form as might make it worthiest of profound and perpetual study by the light of far other lamps than illuminate the stage. Of all vulgar errors the most wanton, the most wilful, and the most resolutely tenacious of life, is that belief bequeathed from the days of Pope, in which it was pardonable, to the days of Mr. Carlyle, in which it is not excusable, to the effect that Shakespeare threw off **Hamlet** as an eagle may moult a feather or a fool may break a jest; that he dropped his work as a bird may drop an egg or a sophist a fallacy; that he wrote "for gain, not glory," or that having written **Hamlet** he thought it nothing very wonderful to have written. For himself to have written, he possibly, nay probably, did not think it anything miraculous; but that he was in the fullest degree conscious of its wonderful positive worth to all men for all time, we have the best evidence possible—his own; and that not by mere word of mouth but by actual stroke of hand. Ben Jonson might shout aloud over his own work on a public stage, "By God 'tis good," and so for all its real goodness and his real greatness make sure that both the workman and his work should be less unnaturally than unreasonably laughed at; Shakespeare knew a better way of showing confidence in himself, but he showed not a whit less confidence. Scene by scene, line for line, stroke upon stroke and touch after touch, he went over all the old laboured ground again; and not to ensure success in his own day and fill his pockets with contemporary pence, but merely and wholly with a purpose to make it worthy of himself and his future students. Pence and praise enough it had evidently brought him in from the first. No more palpable proof of this can be desired than the instantaneous attacks on it, the jeers, howls, hoots and hisses of which a careful ear may catch some far faint echo even yet; the fearful and furtive yelp from beneath of the masked and writhing poeticule, the shrill reverberation all around it of plagiarism and parody. Not one single alteration in the whole play can possibly have been made with a view to stage effect or to present popularity and profit; or we must suppose that Shakespeare, however great as a man, was naturally even greater as a fool. There is a class of mortals to whom this inference is always grateful—to whom the fond belief that every great man must needs be a great fool would seem always to afford real comfort and support: happy, in Prior's phrase, could their inverted rule prove every great fool to be a great man. Every change in the text of ***Hamlet*** has impaired its fitness for the stage and increased its value for the closet in exact and perfect proportion. Now, this is not a matter of opinion—of Mr. Pope's opinion or Mr, Carlyle's; it is a matter of fact and evidence. Even in Shakespeare's time the actors threw out his additions; they throw out these very same additions in our own. The one especial speech, if any one such especial speech there be, in which the personal genius of Shakespeare soars up to the very highest of its height and strikes down to the very deepest of its depth, is passed, over by modern actors; it was cut away by Hemings and Condell. We may almost assume it as certain that no boards have ever echoed—at least, more than once or twice—to the supreme soliloquy of Hamlet. Those words which combine the noblest pleading ever proffered for the rights of human reason with the loftiest vindication ever uttered of those rights, no mortal ear within our knowledge has ever heard spoken on the stage. A convocation even of all priests could not have been more unhesitatingly unanimous in its rejection than seems to have been the hereditary verdict of all actors. It could hardly have been found worthier of theological than it has been found of theatrical condemnation. Yet, beyond all question, magnificent as is that monologue on suicide and doubt which has passed from a proverb into a byword, it is actually eclipsed and distanced at once on philosophic and on poetical grounds by the later soliloquy on reason and resolution.

That Shakespeare was in the genuine sense—that is, in the best and highest and widest meaning of the term—a free thinker, this otherwise practically and avowedly superfluous effusion of all inmost thought appears to me to supply full and sufficient evidence for the conviction of every candid and rational man. To that loftiest and most righteous title which any just and reasoning soul can ever deserve to claim, the greatest save one of all poetic thinkers has thus made good his right for ever.

I trust it will be taken as no breach of my past pledge to abstain from all intrusion on the sacred ground of Gigadibs and the Germans, if I venture to indicate a touch inserted by Shakespeare for no other perceptible or conceivable purpose than to obviate by anticipation the indomitable and ineradicable fallacy of criticism which would find the keynote of Hamlet's character in the quality of irresolution. I may observe at once that the misconception involved in such a reading of the riddle ought to have been evident even without this episodical stroke of illustration. In any case it should be plain to any reader that the signal characteristic of Hamlet's inmost nature is by no means irresolution or hesitation or any form of weakness, but rather the strong conflux of contending forces. That during four whole acts Hamlet cannot or does not make up his mind to any direct and deliberate action against his uncle is true enough; true, also, we may say, that Hamlet had somewhat more of mind than another man to make up, and might properly want somewhat more time than might another man to do it in; but not, I venture to say in spite of Goethe, through innate inadequacy to his task and unconquerable weakness of the will; not, I venture to think in spite of Hugo, through immedicable scepticism of the spirit and irremediable propensity to nebulous intellectual refinement. One practical point in the action of the play precludes us from accepting so ready a solution of the riddle as is suggested either by the simple theory of half-heartedness or by the simple hypothesis of doubt. There is absolutely no other reason, we might say there was no other excuse, for the introduction or intrusion of an else superfluous episode into a play which was already, and which remains even after all possible excisions, one of the longest plays on record. The compulsory expedition of Hamlet to England, his discovery by the way of the plot laid against his life, his interception of the King's letter and his forgery of a substitute for it against the lives of the King's agents, the ensuing adventure of the sea-fight, with Hamlet's daring act of hot-headed personal intrepidity, his capture and subsequent release on terms giving no less patent proof of his cool-headed and ready-witted courage and resource than the attack had afforded of his physically impulsive and even impetuous hardihood—all this serves no purpose whatever but that of exhibiting the instant and almost unscrupulous resolution of Hamlet's character in time of practical need. But for all that he or Hamlet has got by it, Shakespeare might too evidently have spared his pains; and for all this voice as of one crying in a wilderness, Hamlet will too surely remain to the majority of students, not less than to all actors and all editors and all critics, the standing type and embodied emblem of irresolution, half-heartedness, and doubt.

That Hamlet should seem at times to accept for himself, and even to enforce by reiteration of argument upon his conscience and his reason, some such conviction or suspicion as to his own character, tells much rather in disfavour than in favour of its truth. A man whose natural temptation was to swerve, whose inborn inclination was to shrink and skulk aside from duty and from action, would hardly be the first and last person to suspect his own weakness, the one only unbiassed judge and witness of sufficiently sharp-sighted candour and accuracy to estimate aright his poverty of nature and the malformation of his mind. But the high-hearted and tender-conscienced Hamlet, with his native bias towards introspection intensified and inflamed and directed and dilated at once by one imperative pressure and oppression of unavoidable and unalterable circumstance, was assuredly and exactly the one only man to be troubled by any momentary fear that such might indeed be the solution of his riddle, and to feel or to fancy for the moment some kind of ease and relief in the sense of that very trouble. A born doubter would have doubted even of Horatio; hardly can all positive and almost palpable evidence of underhand instigation and inspired good intentions induce Hamlet for some time to doubt even of Ophelia.

III

THE entrance to the third period of Shakespeare is like the entrance to that lost and lesser Paradise of old,

With dreadful faces thronged, and fiery arms.

Lear, Othello, Macbeth, Coriolanus, Antony, Timon, these are names indeed of something more than tragic purport. Only in the sunnier distance beyond, where the sunset of Shakespeare's imagination seems to melt or flow back into the sunrise, do we discern Prospero beside Miranda, Florizel by Perdita, Palamon with Arcite, the same knightly and kindly Duke Theseus as of old; and above them all, and all others of his divine and human children, the crowning and final and ineffable figure of Imogen.

Of all Shakespeare's plays, **King Lear** is unquestionably that in which he has come nearest to the height and to the likeness of the one tragic poet on any side greater than himself whom the world in all its ages has ever seen born of time. It is by far the most Æchylean of his works; the most elemental and primæval, the most oceanic and Titanic in conception. He deals here with no subtleties as in ***Hamlet,*** with no conventions as in ***Othello:*** there is no question of "a divided duty" or a problem half insoluble, a matter of country and connection, of family or of race; we look upward and downward, and in vain, into the deepest things of nature, into the highest things of providence; to the roots of life, and to the stars; from the roots that no God waters to the stars which give no man light; over a world full of death and life without resting-place or guidance.

But in one main point it differs radically from the work and the spirit of Æschylus. Its fatalism is of a darker and harder nature. To Prometheus the fetters of the lord and enemy of mankind were bitter; upon Orestes the hand of heaven was laid too heavily to bear; yet in the not utterly infinite or everlasting distance we see beyond them the promise of the morning on which mystery and justice shall be made one; when righteousness and omnipotence at last shall kiss each other. But on the horizon of Shakespeare's tragic fatalism we see no such twilight of atonement, such pledge of reconciliation as this. Requital, redemption, amends, equity, explanation, pity and mercy, are words without a meaning here.

As flies to wanton boys are we to the gods;
They kill us for their sport.

Here is no need of the Eumenides, children of Night everlasting; for here is very Night herself.

The words just cited are not casual or episodical; they strike the keynote of the whole poem, lay the keystone of the whole arch of thought. There is no contest of conflicting forces, no judgment so much as by casting of lots: far less is there any light of heavenly harmony or of heavenly wisdom, of Apollo or Athene from above. We have heard much and often from theologians of the light of revelation: and some such thing indeed we find in Æschylus: but the darkness of revelation is here.

For in this the most terrible work of human genius it is with the very springs and sources of nature that her student has set himself to deal. The veil of the temple of our humanity is rent in twain. Nature herself, we might say, is revealed—and revealed as unnatural. In face of such a world as this a man might be forgiven who should pray that chaos might come again. Nowhere else in Shakespeare's work or in the universe of jarring lives are the lines of character and event so broadly drawn or so sharply cut. Only the supreme self-command of this one poet could so mould and handle such types as to restrain and prevent their passing from the abnormal into the monstrous; yet even as much as this, at least in all cases but one, it surely has accomplished. In Regan alone would it be, I think, impossible to find a touch or trace of anything less vile than it was devilish. Even Goneril has her one splendid hour, her fire-flaught of hellish glory; when she treads under foot the half-hearted goodness, the wordy and windy though sincere abhorrence, which is all that the mild and impotent revolt of Albany can bring to bear against her imperious and dauntless devilhood; when she flaunts before the eyes of her "milk-livered" and "moral fool" the coming banners of France about the "plumed helm" of his slayer.

On the other side, Kent is the exception which answers to Regan on this. Cordelia, the brotherless Antigone of our stage, has one passing touch of intolerance for what her sister was afterwards to brand as indiscretion and dotage in their father, which redeems her from the charge of perfection. Like Imogen, she is not too inhumanly divine for the sense of divine irritation. Godlike though they be, their very godhead is human and feminine; and only therefore credible, and only therefore adorable. Cloten and Regan, Goneril and Iachimo, have power to stir and embitter the sweetness of their blood. But for the contrast and even the contact of antagonists as abominable as these, the gold of their spirit would be too refined, the lily of their holiness too radiant, the violet of their virtue too sweet. As it is, Shakespeare has gone down perforce among the blackest and the basest things of nature to find anything so equally exceptional in evil as properly to counterbalance and make bearable the excellence and extremity of their goodness. No otherwise could either angel have escaped the blame implied in the very attribute and epithet of blameless. But where the possible depth of human hell is so foul and unfathomable as it appears in the spirits which serve as foils to these, we may endure that in them the inner height of heaven should be no less immaculate and immeasurable.

It should be a truism wellnigh as musty as Hamlet's half cited proverb, to enlarge upon the evidence given in ***King Lear*** of a sympathy with the mass of social misery more wide and deep and direct and bitter and tender than Shakespeare has shown elsewhere. But as even to this day and even in respectable quarters the murmur is not quite duly extinct which would charge on Shakespeare a certain share of divine indifference to suffering, of godlike satisfaction and a less than compassionate content, it is not yet perhaps utterly superfluous to insist on the utter fallacy and falsity of their creed who whether in praise or in blame would rank him to his credit or discredit among such poets as on this side at least may be classed rather with Goethe than with Shelley and with Gautier than with Hugo. A poet of revolution he is not, as none of his country in that generation could have been: but as surely as the author of Julius Cæsar ***has approved himself in the best and highest sense of the word at least potentially a republican, so surely has the author of*** King Lear avowed himself in the only good and rational sense of the words a spiritual if not a political democrat and socialist

It is only, I think, in this most tragic of tragedies that the sovereign lord and incarnate god of pity and terror can be said to have struck with all his strength a chord of which the resonance could excite such angry agony and heartbreak of wrath as that of the brother kings when they smote their staffs against the ground in fierce imperious anguish of agonised and rebellious compassion, at the oracular cry of Calchas for the innocent blood of Iphigenia. The doom even of Desdemona seems as much less morally intolerable as it is more logically inevitable than the doom of Cordelia. But doubtless the fatalism of ***Othello*** is as much darker and harder than that of any third among the plays of Shakespeare, as it is less dark and hard than the fatalism of ***King Lear.*** For upon the head of the very noblest man whom even omnipotence or Shakespeare could ever call to life he has laid a burden in one sense yet heavier than the burden of Lear, insomuch as the sufferer can with somewhat less confidence of universal appeal proclaim himself a man more sinned against than sinning.

And yet, if ever man after Lear might lift up his voice in that protest, it would assuredly be none other than Othello. He is in all the prosperous days of his labour and his triumph so utterly and wholly nobler than the self-centred and wayward king, that the capture of his soul and body in the unimaginable snare of Iago seems a yet blinder and more unrighteous blow

Struck by the envious wrath of man or God

than ever fell on the old white head of that child-changed father. But at least he is destroyed by the stroke of a mightier hand than theirs who struck down Lear. As surely as Othello is the noblest man of man's making, Iago is the most perfect evil-doer, the most potent demi-devil. It is of course the merest commonplace to say as much, and would be no less a waste of speech to add the half comfortable reflection that it is in any case no shame to fall by such a hand. But this subtlest and strangest work of Shakespeare's admits and requires some closer than common scrutiny. Coleridge has admirably described the first great soliloquy which opens to us the pit of hell within as "the motive-hunting of a motiveless malignity." But subtle and profound and just as is this definitive appreciation, there is more in the matter yet than even this. It is not only that Iago, so to speak, half tries to make himself half believe that Othello has wronged him, and that the thought of it gnaws him inly like a poisonous mineral: though this also be true, it is not half the truth—nor half that half again. Malignant as he is, the very subtlest and strongest component of his complex nature is not even malignity. It is the instinct of what Mr. Carlyle would call an inarticulate poet. In his immortal study on the affair of the diamond necklace, the most profound and potent humourist of his country in his century has unwittingly touched on the mainspring of Iago's character—"the very pulse of the machine." He describes his Circe de la Mothe-Valois as a practical dramatic poet or playwright at least in lieu of play-writer: while indicating how and wherefore, with all her constructive skill and rhythmic art in action, such genius as hers so differs from the genius of Shakespeare that she undeniably could not have written a **Hamlet.** Neither could Iago have written an **Othello.** (From this theorem, by the way, a reasoner or a casuist benighted enough to prefer articulate poets to inarticulate, Shakespeare to Cromwell, a fair Vittoria Colonna to a "foul Circe-Megæra," and even such a strategist as Homer to such a strategist as Frederic-William, would not illogically draw such conclusions or infer such corollaries as might result in opinions hardly consonant with the Teutonic-Titanic evangel of the preacher who supplied him with his thesis.) "But what he can do, that he will": and if it be better to make a tragedy than to write one, to act a poem than to sing it, we must allow to Iago a station in the hierarchy of poets very far in advance of his creator's. None of the great inarticulate may more justly claim place and precedence. With all his poetic gift, he has no poetic weakness. Almost any creator but his would have given him some grain of spite or some spark of lust after Desdemona. To Shakespeare's Iago she is no more than is a rhyme to another and articulate poet. [Note 1: What would at least be partly lust in another man is all but purely hatred in Iago.

Now I do love her too:
Not out of absolute lust, (though, peradventure, I stand accountant for as great a sin)
But partly led to diet my revenge.

For "partly "read "wholly," and for "peradventure "read "assuredly," and the incarnate father of lies, made manifest in the flesh, here speaks all but all the truth for once, to himself alone.]. His stanza must at any rate and at all costs be polished: to borrow the metaphor used by Mr. Carlyle in apologetic illustration of a royal hero's peculiar system of levying recruits for his colossal brigade. He has within him a sense or conscience of power incomparable: and this power shall not be left, in Hamlet's phrase, "to fust in him unused" A genuine and thorough capacity for human lust or hate would diminish and degrade the supremacy of his evil. He is almost as far above or beyond vice as he is beneath or beyond virtue. And this it is that makes him impregnable and invulnerable. When once he has said it, we know as well as he that thenceforth he never will speak word. We could smile almost as we can see him to have smiled at Gratiano's most ignorant and empty threat, being well assured that torments will in no wise ope his lips: that as surely and as truthfully as ever did the tortured philosopher before him, he might have told his tormentors that they did but bruise the coating, batter the crust, or break the shell of Iago. Could we imagine a far other lost spirit than Farinata degli Uberti's endowed with Farinata's might of will, and transferred from the sepulchres of fire to the dykes of Malebolge, we might conceive something of Iago's attitude in hell—of his unalterable and indomitable posture for all eternity. As though it were possible and necessary that in some one point the extremities of all conceivable good and of all imaginable evil should meet and mix together in a new "marriage of heaven and hell," the action in passion of the most devilish among all the human damned could hardly be other than that of the most godlike among all divine saviours—the figure of Iago than a reflection by hell-fire of the figure of Prometheus.

Between Iago and Othello the position of Desdemona is precisely that defined with such quaint sublimity of fancy in the old English by-word—"between the devil and the deep sea." Deep and pure and strong and adorable always and terrible and pitiless on occasion as the sea is the great soul of the glorious hero to whom she has given herself; and what likeness of man's enemy from Satan down to Mephistopheles could be matched for danger and for dread against the good bluff soldierly trustworthy figure of honest Iago? The rough license of his tongue at once takes warrant from his good soldiership and again gives warrant for his honesty: so that in a double sense it does him yeoman's service, and that twice told. It is pitifully ludicrous to see him staged to the show like a member—and a very inefficient member—of the secret police. But it would seem impossible for actors to understand that he is not a would-be detective, an aspirant for the honours of a Vidocq, a candidate for the laurels of a Vautrin: that he is no less than Lepidus, or than Antony's horse, "a tried and valiant soldier." It is perhaps natural that the two deepest and subtlest of all Shakespeare's intellectual studies in good and evil should be the two most painfully misused and misunderstood alike by his commentators and his fellows of the stage: it is certainly undeniable that no third figure of his creation has ever been on both sides as persistently misconceived and misrepresented with such desperate pertinacity as Hamlet and Iago.

And it is only when Iago is justly appreciated that we can justly appreciate either Othello or Desdemona. This again should surely be no more than the truism that it sounds; but practically it would seem to be no less than an adventurous and audacious paradox. Remove or deform or diminish or modify the dominant features of the destroyer, and we have but the eternal and vulgar figures of jealousy and innocence, newly vamped and veneered and padded and patched up for the stalest purposes of puppetry. As it is, when Coleridge asks "which do we pity the most" at the fall of the curtain, we can surely answer, Othello. Noble as are the "most blessed conditions" of "the gentle Desdemona," he is yet the nobler of the two; and has suffered more in one single pang than she could suffer in life or in death.

But if **Othello** be the most pathetic, **King Lear** the most terrible, **Hamlet** the subtlest and deepest work of Shakespeare, the highest in abrupt and steep simplicity of epic tragedy is **Macbeth.** There needs no ghost come from the grave, any reader may too probably remark, to tell us this. But in the present generation such novelties have been unearthed regarding Shakespeare that the reassertion of an old truth may seem to have upon it some glittering reflection from the brazen brightness of a brand-new lie. Have not certain wise men of the east of England—Cantabrigian Magi, led by the star of their goddess Mathesis ("mad Mathesis," as a daring poet was once ill-advised enough to dub her doubtful deity in defiance of scansion rather than of truth)—have they not detected in the very heart of this tragedy the "paddling palms and pinching fingers" of Thomas Middleton?

To the simpler eyes of less learned Thebans than these—Thebes, by the way, was Dryden's irreverent name for Cambridge, the nursing mother of "his green unknowing youth," when that "renegade" was recreant enough to compliment Oxford at her expense as the chosen Athens of "his riper age"—the likelihood is only too evident that the sole text we possess of **Macbeth** has not been interpolated but mutilated. In their version of **Othello,** remarkably enough, the "player-editors," contrary to their wont, have added to the treasure-house of their text one of the most precious jewels that ever the prodigal afterthought of a great poet bestowed upon the rapture of his readers. Some of these, by way of thanksgiving, have complained with a touch of petulance that it was out of place and superfluous in the setting: nay, that it was incongruous with all the circumstances—out of tone and out of harmony and out of keeping with character and tune and time. In other lips indeed than Othello's, at the crowning minute of culminant agony, the rush of imaginative reminiscence which brings back upon his eyes and ears the lightning foam and tideless thunder of the Pontic sea might seem a thing less natural than sublime. But Othello has the passion of a poet closed in as it were and shut up behind the passion of a hero. For all his practical readiness of martial eye and ruling hand in action, he is also in his season "of imagination all compact." Therefore it is that in the face and teeth of all devils akin to Iago that hell could send forth to hiss at her election, we feel and recognise the spotless exaltation, the sublime and sunbright purity, of Desdemona's inevitable and invulnerable love. When once we likewise have seen Othello's visage in his mind, we see too how much more of greatness is in this mind than in another hero's. For such an one, even a boy may well think how thankfully and joyfully he would lay down his life. Other friends we have of Shakespeare's giving whom we love deeply and well, if hardly with such love as could weep for him all the tears of the body and all the blood of the heart: but there is none we love like Othello.

I must part from his presence again for a season, and return to my topic in the text of *Macbeth.* That it is piteously rent and ragged and clipped and garbled in some of its earlier scenes, the rough construction and the poltfoot metre, lame sense and limping verse, each maimed and mangled subject of players' and printers' most treasonable tyranny-contending as it were to seem harsher than the other, combine in this contention to bear indisputable and intolerable witness. Only where the witches are, and one more potent and more terrible than all witches and all devils at their beck, can we be sure that such traitors have not robbed us of one touch from Shakespeare's hand. The second scene of the play at least bears marks of such handling as the brutal Shakespearean Hector's of the "mangled Myrmidons"; it is too visibly "noseless, handless, hacked and chipped" as it comes to us, crying on Hemings and Condell. And it is in this unlucky scene that unkindly criticism has not unsuccessfully sought for the gravest faults of language and manner to be found in Shakespeare. For certainly it cannot be cleared from the charge of a style stiffened and swollen with clumsy braid and crabbed bombast. But against the weird sisters, and her who sits above them and apart, more awful than Hecate's very self, no mangling hand has been stretched forth; no blight of mistranslation by perversion has fallen upon the words which interpret and expound the hidden things of their evil will.

To one tragedy as to one comedy of Shakespeare's, the casual or the natural union of especial popularity with especial simplicity in selection and in treatment of character makes it as superfluous as it would be difficult to attempt any application of analytical criticism. There is nothing in them of a nature so compound or so complex as to call for solution or resolution into its primal elements. Here there is some genuine ground for the generally baseless and delusive opinion of self-complacent sciolism that he who runs may read Shakespeare. These two plays it is hardly worth while to point out by name: all probable readers will know them at once for **Macbeth** and *As You Like It.* There can hardly be a single point of incident or of character on which the youngest reader will not find himself at one with the oldest, the dullest with the brightest among the scholars of Shakespeare. It would be an equal waste of working hours or of playtime if any of these should devote any part of either a whole-schoolday or a holiday to remark or to rhapsody on the character of Macbeth or of Orlando, of Rosalind or of Lady Macbeth. He that runs, let him read: and he that has ears, let him hear.

I cannot but think that enough at least of time has been spent if not wasted by able and even by eminent men on examination of **Coriolanus** with regard to its political aspect or bearing upon social questions. It is from first to last, for all its turmoil of battle and clamour of contentious factions, rather a private and domestic than a public or historical tragedy. As in fulius Cæsar the family had been so wholly subordinated to the state, and all personal interests so utterly dominated by the preponderance of national duties, that even the sweet and sublime figure of Portia passing in her "awful loveliness" was but as a profile half caught in the background of an episode, so here on the contrary the whole force of the final impression is not that of a conflict between patrician and plebeian, but solely that of a match of passions played out for life and death between a mother and a son. The partisans of oligarchic or democratic systems may wrangle at their will over the supposed evidences of Shakespeare's prejudice against this creed and prepossession in favour of that: a third bystander may rejoice in the proof thus established of his impartial indifference towards either: it is all nothing to the real point in hand. The subject of the whole play is not the exile's revolt, the rebel's repentance, or the traitor's reward, but above all it is the son's tragedy. The inscription on the plinth of this tragic statue is simply to Volumnia Victrix.

A loftier or a more perfect piece of man's work was never done in all the world than this tragedy of ***Coriolanus:*** the one fit and crowning epithet for its companion or successor is that bestowed by Coleridge—"the most wonderful." It would seem a sign or birthmark of only the greatest among poets that they should be sure to rise instantly for awhile above the very highest of their native height at the touch of a thought of Cleopatra. So was it, as we all know, with William Shakespeare: so is it, as we all see, with Victor Hugo. As we feel in the marvellous and matchless verses of ***Zim-Zizimi*** all the splendour and fragrance and miracle of her mere bodily presence, so from her first imperial dawn on the stage of Shakespeare to the setting of that eastern star behind a pall of undissolving cloud we feel the charm and the terror and the mystery of her absolute and royal soul. Byron wrote once to Moore, with how much truth or sincerity those may guess who would care to know, that his friend's first "confounded book" of thin prurient jingle ("we call it a mellisonant tingle-tangle," as Randolph's mock Oberon says of a stolen sheep-bell) had been the first cause of all his erratic or erotic frailties: it is not impossible that spirits of another sort may remember that to their own innocent infantine perceptions the first obscure electric revelation of what Blake calls "the Eternal Female" was given through a blind wondering thrill of childish rapture by a lightning on the baby dawn of their senses and their soul from the sunrise of Shakespeare's Cleopatra.

Never has he given such proof of his incomparable instinct for abstinence from the wrong thing as well as achievement of the right. He has utterly rejected and disdained all occasion of setting her off by means of any lesser foil than all the glory of the world with all its empires. And we need not Antony's example to show us that these are less than straws in the balance.

Entre elle et l'univers qui s'offraient à la fols
Il hésita, lâchant le monde dans son choix.

Even as that Roman grasp relaxed and let fall the world, so has Shakespeare's self let go for awhile his greater world of imagination, with all its all but infinite variety of life and thought and action, for love of that more infinite variety which custom could not stale. Himself a second and a yet more fortunate Antony, he has once more laid a world, and a world more wonderful than ever, at her feet. He has put aside for her sake all other forms and figures of womanhood; he, father or creator of Rosalind, of Cordelia, of Desdemona, and of Imogen, he too, like the sungod and sender of all song, has anchored his eyes on her whom "Phœbus' amorous pinches" could not leave "black," nor "wrinkled deep in time"; on that incarnate and imperishable "spirit of sense," to whom at the very last

> The stroke of death is as a lover's pinch,
> That hurts, and is desired.

To him, as to the dying husband of Octavia, this creature of his own hand might have boasted herself that the loveliest and purest among all her sisters of his begetting.

> with her modest eyes
> And still conclusion, shall acquire no honour,
> Demurring upon me.

To sum up, Shakespeare has elsewhere given us in ideal incarnation the perfect mother, the perfect wife, the perfect daughter, the perfect mistress, or the perfect maiden: here only once for all he has given us the perfect and the everlasting woman.

And what a world of great men and great things, "high actions and high passions," is this that he has spread under her for a footcloth or hung behind her for a curtain! The descendant of that other his ancestral Alcides, late offshoot of the god whom he loved and who so long was loth to leave him, is here as in history the visible one man revealed who could grapple for a second with very Rome and seem to throw it, more lightly than he could cope with Cleopatra. And not the

Roman Landor himself could see or make us see more clearly than has his fellow provincial of Warwickshire that first imperial nephew of her great first paramour, who was to his actual uncle even such a foil and counterfeit and perverse and prosperous parody as the son of Hortense Beauharnais of Saint Leu to the son of Letizia Buonaparte of Ajaccio. For Shakespeare too, like Landor, had watched his "sweet Octavius" smilingly and frowningly "draw under nose the knuckle of forefinger" as he looked out upon the trail of innocent blood after the bright receding figure of his brave young kinsman. The fair-faced false "present God" of his poetic parasites, the smooth triumphant patron and preserver with the heart of ice and iron, smiles before us to the very life. It is of no account now to remember that

> he at Philippi kept
> His sword even like a dancer:

for the sword of Antony that struck for him is in the renegade hand of Dercetas.

I have said nothing of Enobarbus or of Eros, the fugitive once ruined by his flight and again redeemed by the death-agony of his dark and doomed repentance, or the freedman transfigured by a death more fair than freedom through the glory of the greatness of his faith: for who can speak of all things or of half that are in Shakespeare? And who can speak worthily of any?

I am come now to that strange part of a task too high for me, where I must needs speak not only (as may indeed well be) unworthily, but also (as may well seem) unlovingly, of some certain portions in the mature and authentic work of Shakespeare. "Though it be honest, it is never good" to do so: yet here I cannot choose but speak plainly after my own poor conscience, and risk all chances of chastisement as fearful as any once threatened for her too faithful messenger by the heart-stricken wrath of Cleopatra.

In the greater part of this third period, taking a swift and general view of it for contrast or comparison of qualities with the second, we constantly find beauty and melody transfigured into harmony and sublimity; an exchange unquestionably for the better: but in certain stages, or only perhaps in a single stage of it, we frequently find humour and reality supplanted by realism and obscenity; an exchange undeniably for the worse. The note of his earliest comic style was often a boyish or a birdlike wantonness, very capable of such liberties and levities as those of Lesbia's sparrow with the lip or bosom of his mistress; as notably in the parts of Boyet and Mercutio: and indeed there is a bright vein of mere wordy wilfulness running throughout the golden youth of the two plays which connects **Love's Labour's Lost** with **Romeo and Juliet** as by a thread of floss silk not always "most excellently ravelled," nor often unspotted or unentangled. In the second period this gaiety was replaced by the utmost frankness and fullness of humour, as a boy's merry madness by the witty wisdom of a man: but now for a time it would seem as if the good comic qualities of either period were displaced and ousted by mere coarseness and crudity like that of a hard harsh photograph. This ultra-Circean transformation of spirit and brutification of speech we do not find in the lighter interludes of great and perfect tragedy: for the porter in **Macbeth** makes hardly an exception worth naming. It is when we come upon the singular little group of two or three plays not accurately definable at all but roughly describable as tragicomedies, or more properly in two cases at least as tragedies docked of their natural end, curtailed of the due catastrophe—it is then that we find for the swift sad bright lightnings of laughter from the lips of the sweet and bitter fool whose timeless disappearance from the stage of **King Lear** seems for once a sure sign of inexplicable weariness or forgetfulness on Shakespeare's part, so nauseous and so sorry a substitute as the fetid fun and rancid ribaldry of Pandarus and Thersites. I must have leave to say that the coincidence of these two in the scheme of a single play is a thing hardly bearable by men who object to too strong a savour of those too truly "Eternal Cesspools" over which the first of living humourists holds as it were for ever an everlasting nose—or rather, in one sense, does not hold but expand it for the fuller inhalation of their too congenial fumes with an apparent relish which will always seem the most deplorable to those who the most gratefully and reasonably admire that high heroic genius, for love of which the wiser sort of men must finally forgive all the noisy aberrations of his misanthropy and philobulgary, anti-Gallican and Russolatrous insanities of perverse and morbid eloquence.

The three detached or misclassified plays of Shakespeare in which alone a reverent and reasonable critic might perhaps find something rationally and really exceptionable have also this far other quality in common, that in them as in his topmost tragedies of the same period either the exaltation of his eloquence touches the very highest point of expressible poetry, or his power of speculation alternately sounds the gulfs and scales the summits of all imaginable thought. In all three of them the power of passionate and imaginative eloquence is not only equal in spirit or essence but identical in figure or in form: in those two of them which deal almost as much with speculative intelligence as with poetic action and passion, the tones and methods, types and objects of thought, are also not equal only but identical. An all but absolute brotherhood in thought and style and tone and feeling unites the quasi-tragedy of ***Troilus and Cressida*** with what in the lamentable default of as apt a phrase in English I must call by its proper designation in French the tragédie manqué *of* Measure for Measure. ***In the simply romantic fragment of the Shakespearean*** Pericles, where there was no call and no place for the poetry of speculative or philosophic intelligence, there is the same positive and unmistakable identity of imaginative and passionate style.

I cannot but conjecture that the habitual students of Shakespeare's printed plays must have felt startled as by something of a shock when the same year exposed for the expenditure of their sixpences two reasonably correct editions of a play unknown to the boards in the likeness of ***Troilus and Cressida*** side by side or cheek by jowl with a most unreasonably and unconscionably incorrect issue of a much older stage favourite, now newly beautified and fortified, in ***Pericles Prince of Tyre.*** Hitherto, ever since the appearance of his first poem, and its instant acceptance by all classes from courtiers to courtesans under a somewhat dubious and two headed form of popular success,—'vrai succés de scandale s'il en fut'—even the potent influence and unequivocal example of Rabelais had never once even in passing or in seeming affected or infected the progressive and triumphal genius of Shakespeare with a taint or touch of any thing offensive to healthier and cleanlier organs of perception than such as may belong to a genuine or a pretending Puritan. But on taking in his hand that one of these two new dramatic pamphlets which might first attract him either by its double novelty as a never acted play or by a title of yet more poetic and romantic associations than its fellow's, such a purchaser as I have supposed, with his mind full of the sweet rich fresh humour which he would feel a right to expect from Shakespeare, could hardly have undergone less than a qualm or a pang of strong disrelish and distaste on finding one of the two leading comic figures of the play break in upon it at his entrance not even with "a fool-born jest," but with full-mouthed and foul-mouthed effusion of such rank and rancorous personalities as might properly pollute the lips even of some emulous descendant or antiquarian reincarnation of Thersites, on application or even apprehension of a whip cracked in passing over the assembled heads of a pseudocritical and mock-historic society. In either case we moderns at least might haply desire the intervention of a beadle's hand as heavy and a sceptral cudgel as knotty as ever the son of Laertes applied to the shoulders of the first of the type or the tribe of Thersites. For this brutal and brutish buffoon—I am speaking of Shakespeare's Thersites—has no touch of humour in all his currish composition: Shakespeare had none as nature has none to spare for such dirty dogs as those of his kind or generation. There is not even what Coleridge with such exquisite happiness defined as being the quintessential property of Swift—"anima Rabelæsii habitans in sicco—the soul of Rabelais dwelling in a dry place." It is the fallen soul of Swift himself at its lowest, dwelling in a place yet drier: the familiar spirit or less than Socratic dæmon of the Dean informing the genius of Shakespeare. And thus for awhile infected and possessed, the divine genius had not power to re-inform and re-create the daemonic spirit by virtue of its own clear essence. This wonderful play, one of the most admirable among all the works of Shakespeare's immeasurable and unfathomable intelligence, as it must always hold its natural high place among the most admired, will always in all probability be also and as naturally, the least beloved of all. It would be as easy and as profitable a problem to solve the Rabelaisian riddle of the bombinating chimæra with its potential or hypothetical faculty of deriving sustenance from a course of diet on second intentions, as to read the riddle of Shakespeare's design in the procreation of this yet more mysterious and magnificent monster of a play. That on its production in print it was formally announced as "a new play never staled with the stage, never clapper-clawed with the palms of the vulgar," we know; must we infer or may we suppose that therefore it was not originally written for the stage? Not all plays were which even at that date appeared in print: yet it would seem something more than strange that one such play, written simply for the study, should have been the extra-professional work of Shakespeare: and yet again it would seem stranger that he should have designed this prodigious nondescript or portent of supreme genius for the public stage: and strangest of all, if so, that he should have so designed it in vain. Perhaps after all a better than any German or Germanising commentary on the subject would be the simple and summary ejaculation of Celia—"O wonderful, wonderful, and most wonderful wonderful, and yet again wonderful, and after that out of all whooping!" The perplexities of the whole matter seem literally to crowd and thicken upon us at every step. What ailed the man or any man to write such a manner of dramatic poem at all? and having written, to keep it beside him or let it out of his hands into stranger and more slippery keeping, unacted and unprinted? A German will rush in with an answer where an Englishman (non angelus sed Anglus) will naturally fear to tread.

Alike in its most palpable perplexities and in its most patent splendours, this political and philosophic and poetic problem, this hybrid and hundred-faced and hydra-headed prodigy, at once defies and derides all definitive comment. This however we may surely and confidently say of it, that of all Shakespeare's offspring it is the one whose best things lose least by extraction and separation from their context. That some cynic had lately bitten him by the brain—and possibly a cynic himself in a nearly rabid stage of anthropophobia—we might conclude as reasonably from consideration of the whole as from examination of the parts more especially and virulently affected: yet how much is here also of hyper-Platonic subtlety and sublimity, of golden and Hyblæan eloquence above the reach and beyond the snap of any cynic's tooth! Shakespeare, as under the guidance at once for good and for evil of his alternately Socratic and Swiftian familiar, has set himself as if prepensely and on purpose to brutalise the type of Achilles and spiritualise the type of Ulysses. The former is an enterprise never to be utterly forgiven by any one who ever loved from the very birth of his boyhood the very name of the son of the sea-goddess: in the glorious words of Mr. Browning's young first-born poem,

Who stood beside the naked Swift-footed,

And bound [his] forehead with Proserpine's hair.

It is true, if that be any little compensation, that Hector and Andromache fare here hardly better than he: while of the momentary presentation of Helen on the dirtier boards of a stage more miry than the tub of Diogenes I would not if I could and I must not though I would say so much as one single proper word. The hysterics of the eponymous hero and the harlotries of the eponymous heroine remove both alike beyond the outer pale of all rational and manly sympathy; though Shakespeare's self may never have exceeded or equalled for subtle and accurate and bitter fidelity the study here given of an utterly light woman, shallow and loose and dissolute in the most literal sense, rather than perverse or unkindly or unclean; and though Keats alone in his most perfect mood of lyric passion and burning vision as full of fragrance as of flame could have matched and all but overmatched those passages in which the rapture of Troilus makes pale and humble by comparison the keenest raptures of Romeo.

The relative disfavour in which the play of **Measure for Measure** has doubtless been at all times generally held is not in my opinion simply explicable on the theory which of late years has been so powerfully and plausibly advanced and advocated on the highest poetic or judicial authority in France or in the world, that in the land of many-coloured cant and many-coated hypocrisy the type of Angelo is something too much a prototype or an autotype of the huge national vice of England. This comment is in itself as surely just and true as it is incisive and direct: but it will not cover by any manner of means the whole question. The strong and radical objection distinctly brought forward against this play, and strenuously supported by the wisest and the warmest devotee among all the worshippers of Shakespeare, is not exactly this, that the Puritan Angelo is exposed: it is that the Puritan Angelo is unpunished. In the very words of Coleridge, it is that by his pardon and his marriage "the strong indignant claim of justice" is "baffled." The expression is absolutely correct and apt: justice is not merely evaded or ignored or even defied: she is both in the older and the newer sense of the word directly and deliberately baffled; buffeted, outraged, insulted, struck in the face. We are left hungry and thirsty after having been made to thirst and hunger for some wholesome single grain at least of righteous and too long retarded retribution: we are tricked out of our dole, defeated of our due, lured and led on to look for some equitable and satisfying upshot, defrauded and derided and sent empty away.

That this play is in its very inmost essence a tragedy, and that no sleight of hand or force of hand could give it even a tolerable show of coherence or consistency when clipped and docked of its proper and rightful end, the mere tone of style prevalent throughout all its better parts to the absolute exclusion of any other would of itself most amply suffice to show. Almost all that is here worthy of Shakespeare at any time is worthy of Shakespeare at his highest: and of this every touch, every line, every incident, every syllable, belongs to pure and simple tragedy. The evasion of a tragic end by the invention and intromission of Mariana has deserved and received high praise for its ingenuity: but ingenious evasion of a natural and proper end is usually the distinctive quality which denotes a workman of a very much lower school than the school of Shakespeare. In short and in fact, the whole elaborate machinery by which the complete and completely unsatisfactory result of the whole plot is attained is so thoroughly worthy of such a contriver as "the old fantastical duke of dark corners" as to be in a moral sense, if I dare say what I think, very far from thoroughly worthy of the wisest and mightiest mind that ever was informed with the spirit or genius of creative poetry.

I have one more note to add in passing which touches simply on a musical point in lyric verse; and from which I would therefore give any biped who believes that ears "should be long to measure Shakespeare" all timely warning to avert the length of his own. A very singular question, and one to me unaccountable except by a supposition which on charitable grounds I should be loth to entertain for a moment—namely, that such ears are commoner than I would fain believe on heads externally or ostensibly human,—has been raised with regard to the first immortal song of Mariana in the moated grange. This question is whether the second verse appended by Fletcher to that divine Shakespearean fragment may not haply have been written by the author of the first. The visible and audible evidence that it cannot is of a kind which must at once leap into sight of all human eyes and conviction of all human ears. The metre of Shakespeare's verse, as written by Shakespeare, is not the metre of Fletcher's. It can only seem the same to those who hear by finger and not by ear: a class now at all events but too evidently numerous enough to refute Sir Hugh's antiquated objection to the once apparently tautologous phrase of Pistol. [Note 1: I add the proof in a Note, so as to take tip no more than a small necessary space of my text with the establishment of a fact which yet can seem insignificant to no mortal who has a human ear for lyric song. Shakespeare's verse, as all the wide world knows, ends thus:

But my kisses bring again,
bring again,
Seals of love, but sealed in vain,
sealed in vain.

The echo has been dropped by Fletcher, who has thus achieved the remarkable musical feat of turning a nightingale's note into a sparrow's. The mutilation of Philomela by the hands of Tereus was a jest compared to the mutilation of Shakespeare by the hands of Fletcher: who thereby reduced the close of the first verse into agreement if not into accordance with the close of his own. This appended verse, as all the world does not and need not know, ends thus:

But first set my poor heart free,
Bound in those icy chains by thee.

Even an earless owner of fingers enough to count on may by their help convince himself of the difference in metre here. But not only does the last line, with unsolicited and literally superfluous liberality, offer us a syllable over measure; the words are such as absolutely to defy antiphonal repetition or reverberation of the three last in either line. Let us therefore, like good scriptural scholars, according equally to the letter and the spirit of the text, render unto Fletcher the things which be Fletcher's, and unto Shakespeare the things which be Shakespeare's.]

It is of course inexplicable, but it is equally of course undeniable, that the mention of Shakespeare's **Pericles** would seem immediately and invariably to recall to a virtuous critical public of nice and nasty mind the prose portions of the fourth act, the whole of the prose portions of the fourth act, and nothing but the prose portions of the fourth act To readers and writers of books who readily admit their ineligibility as members of a Society for the Suppression of Shakespeare or Rabelais, of Homer or the Bible, it will seem that the third and fifth acts of this ill-fated and ill-famed play, and with them the poetical parts of the fourth act, are composed of metal incomparably more attractive. But the virtuous critic, after the alleged nature of the vulturine kind, would appear to have eyes and ears and nose for nothing else. It is true that somewhat more of humour, touched once and again with subtler hints of deeper truth, is woven into the too realistic weft of these too lifelike scenes than into any of the corresponding parts in ***Measure for Measure*** or in ***Troilus and Cressida;*** true also that in the hands of imitators, in hands so much weaker than Shakespeare's as were Heywood's or Davenport's (who transplanted this unlovely episode from ***Pericle*** into a play of his own), these very scenes or such as they reappear unredeemed by any such relief in all the rank and rampant ugliness of their raw repulsive realism: true, again, that Fletcher has once equalled them in audacity, while stripping off the nakedness of his subject the last ragged and rude pretence at a moral purpose, and investing it instead with his very brightest robe of gay parti-coloured humour: but after all it remains equally true that to senses less susceptible of attraction by carrion than belong to the vultures of critical and professional virtue they must always remain as they have always been, something very considerably more than unattractive. I at least for one must confess myself insufficiently virtuous to have ever at any time for any moment felt towards them the very slightest touch of any feeling more attractive than repulsion. And herewith I hasten to wash my hands of the only unattractive matter in the only three of Shakespeare's plays which offer any such matter to the perceptions of any healthy-minded and reasonable human creature.

But what now shall I say that may not be too pitifully unworthy of the glories and the beauties, the unsurpassable pathos and sublimity inwoven with the imperial texture of this very play? the blood-red Tyrian purple of tragic maternal jealousy, which might seem to array it in a worthy attire of its Tyrian name; the flower-soft loveliness of maiden lamentation over the flower-strewn seaside grave of Marina's old sea-tossed nurse, where I am unvirtuous enough (as virtue goes among moralists) to feel more at home and better at ease than in the atmosphere of her later lodging in Mitylene? What, above all, shall be said of that storm above all storms ever raised in poetry, which ushered into a world of such wonders and strange chances the daughter of the wave-worn and world-wandering prince of Tyre? Nothing but this perhaps, that it stands—or rather let me say that it blows and sounds and shines and rings and thunders and lightens as far ahead of all others as the burlesque sea-storm of Rabelais beyond all possible storms of comedy. The recent compiler of a most admirably skilful and most delicately invaluable compendium of Pantagruel or manual by way of guidebook to Rabelais has but too justly taken note of the irrefragable evidence there given that the one prose humourist who is to Aristophanes as the human twin-star Castor to Pollux the divine can never have practically weathered an actual gale; but if I may speak from a single experience of one which a witness long inured to Indian storm as well as Indian battle had never seen matched out of the tropics if ever overmatched within them, I should venture to say, were the poet in question any other mortal man than Shakespeare, to whom all things were better known by instinct than ever they can be to others by experience, that the painter of the storm in **Pericles** must have shared the adventure and relished the rapture of such an hour. None other most assuredly than himself alone could have mingled with the material passion of the elements such human passion of pathos as thrills in such tenderly sublime undertone of an agony so nobly subdued through the lament of Pericles over Thaisa. As in his opening speech of this scene we heard all the clangour and resonance of warring wind and sea, so now we hear a sound of sacred and spiritual music as solemn as the central monochord of the inner main itself.

That the three last acts of **Pericles,** with the possible if hot over probable exception of the so-called Chorus, [Note 1: It is worth remark that in a still older sample of an older and ruder form of play than can have been the very earliest mould in which the pristine or pre-Shakespearean model of **Pericles** was cast, the part of Chorus here assigned to Gower was filled by a representative of his fellow-poet Lydgate.] are wholly the work of Shakespeare in the ripest fullness of his latter genius, is a position which needs exactly as much proof as does his single-handed authorship of **Hamlet, Lear, Macbeth** and **Othello.** In the fifth act is a remarkable instance of a thing remarkably rare with him; the recast or repetition in an improved and reinvigorated form of a beautiful image or passage occurring in a previous play. The now only too famous I metaphor of "patience on a monument smiling at grief"—too famous we might call it for its own I fame—is transfigured as from human beauty to divine, in its transformation to the comparison of Marina's look with that of "Patience gazing on kings' graves, and smiling Extremity out of act." A precisely similar parallel is one to which I have referred elsewhere; that between the two passages respectively setting forth the reciprocal love of Helena and Hermia, of Emilia and Flavina. The change of style and spirit in either case of reiteration is the change from a simpler to a sublimer form of beauty.

In the two first acts of **Pericles** there are faint and rare but evident and positive traces of a passing touch from the hasty hand of Shakespeare: even here too we may say after Dido:—

Nec tam aversus equos Tyriâ sol jungit ab urbe.

It has been said that those most unmistakable verses on "the blind mole" are not such as any man could insert into another man's work, or slip in between the lines of an inferior poet: and that they occur naturally enough in a speech of no particular excellence. I take leave decisively to question the former assertion, and flatly to contradict the latter. The pathetic and magnificent lines in dispute do not occur naturally enough, or at all naturally, among the very poor, flat, creeping verses between which they have been thrust with such over freehanded recklessness. No purple patch was ever more pitifully out of place. There is indeed no second example of such wanton and wayward liberality; but the generally lean and barren style of these opening acts does not crawl throughout on exactly the same low level.

The last of the only three plays with which I venture to find any fault on the score of moral taste is the first on my list of the only three plays belonging to this last period on which, as they now stand, I trace the indisputable track of another touch than Shakespeare's. But in the two cases remaining our general task of distinction should on the whole be simple and easy enough for the veriest babes and sucklings in the lower school of Shakespeare.

That the two great posthumous fragments we possess of Shakespeare's uncompleted work are incomplete simply because the labour spent on either was cut short by his timeless death is the first natural assumption of any student with an eye quick enough to catch the point where the traces of his hand break off; but I should now be inclined to guess rather that on reconsideration of the subjects chosen he had rejected or dismissed them for a time at least as unfit for dramatic handling. It could have needed no great expenditure of reasoning or reflection to convince a man of lesser mind and less experience than Shakespeare's that no subject could possibly be more unmanageable, more indomitably improper for such a purpose, than he had selected in *Timon of Athens.* How came ever to fall across such a subject, to hit upon such a choice, we can spend no profitable time or pains in trying to conjecture. It is clear, however, that at all events there was a season when the inexplicable attraction of it was too strong for him to resist the singular temptation to body in palpable form, to array in dramatic payment, to invest with imaginative magnificence, the godless ascetic passion of misanthropy, the martyrdom of an atheistic Stylites. Timon is doubtless a man of far nobler type than any monomaniac of the tribe of Macarius: but his immeasurable superiority in spiritual rank to the hermit fathers of the desert serves merely to make him a thought madder and a grain more miserable than the whole Thebaid of Christomaniacs rolled into one. Foolish and fruitless as it has ever been to hunt through Shakespeare's plays and sonnets on the false scent of a fantastic trail, to put thaumaturgic trust in a dark dream of tracking his untraceable personality through labyrinthine byways of life and visionary crossroads of character, it is yet surely no blind assumption to accept the plain evidence in both so patent before us, that he too like other men had his dark seasons of outer or of inner life, and like other poets found them or made them fruitful as well as bitter, though it might be but of bitter fruit. And of such there is here enough to glut the gorge of all the monks in monkery, or strengthen for a forty days' fast any brutallest unwashed theomaniac of the Thebaid. The most unconscionably unclean of all foul-minded fanatics might have been satisfied with the application to all women from his mother upwards of the monstrous and magnificent obloquy found by Timon as insufficient to overwhelm as his gold was inadequate to satisfy one insatiable and indomitable "brace of harlots." In *Troilus and Cressida* we found too much that Swift might have written when half inspired by the genius of Shakespeare; in the great and terrible fourth act of *Timon* we find such tragedy as Juvenal might have written when half deified by the spirit of Æschylus.

There is a noticeable difference between the case of *Timon* and the two other cases (diverse enough between themselves) of late or mature work but partially assignable to the hand of Shakespeare. In *Pericles* we may know exactly how much was added by Shakespeare to the work of we know not whom; in *The Two Noble Kinsmen* we can tell sometimes to a hair's breadth in a hemistich by whom how much was added to the posthumous text of Shakespeare; in *Timon* we cannot assert with the same confidence in the same accuracy that just so many scenes and no more, just so many speeches and none other, were the work of Shakespeare's or of some other hand. Throughout the first act his presence lightens on us by flashes, as his voice peals out by fits, from behind or above the too meanly decorated altar of tragic or satiric song: in the second it is more sensibly continuous; in the third it is all but utterly eclipsed; in the fourth it is but very rarely intercepted for a very brief interval in the dark divine service of a darker Commination Day: in the fifth it predominates generally over the sullen and brooding atmosphere with the fierce imperious glare of a "bloody sun" like that which the wasting shipmen watched at noon "in a hot and copper sky." There is here no more to say of a poem inspired at once by the triune Furies of Ezekiel, of Juvenal, and of Dante.

I can imagine no reason but that already suggested why Shakespeare should in a double sense have taken Chaucer for his model or example in leaving half told a story which he had borrowed from the father and master of our narrative poetry. Among all competent scholars and all rational students of Shakespeare there can have been, except possibly with regard to three of the shorter scenes, no room for doubt or perplexity oil any detail of the subject since the perfect summary and the masterly decision of Mr. Dyce. These three scenes, as no such reader will need to be told or reminded, are the two first soliloquies of the Gaoler's Daughter after the release of Palamon, and the scene of the portraits, as we may in a double sense call it, in which Emilia, after weighing against each other in solitude the likenesses of the cousins, receives from her own kinsfolk a full and laboured description of their leading champions on either side. Even setting apart for once and for a moment the sovereign evidence of mere style, we must recognise in this last instance a beautiful and significant example of that loyal and loving fidelity to the minor passing suggestions of Chaucer's text which on all possible occasions of such comparison so markedly and vividly distinguishes the work of Shakespeare's from the work of Fletcher's hand. Of the pestilent abuse and perversion to which Fletcher has put the perhaps already superfluous hints or sketches by Shakespeare for an episodical underplot, in his transmutation of Palamon's love-stricken and luckless deliverer into the disgusting burlesque of a mock. Ophelia, I have happily no need as I should certainly have no patience to speak. [Note 1: Except perhaps one little word of due praise for the pretty imitation or recollection of his dead friend Beaumont rather than of Shakespeare, in the description of the crazed girl whose "careless tresses a wreath of bullrush rounded" where she sat playing with flowers for emblems at a game of love and sorrow—but liker in all else to Bellario by another fountain-side than to Ophelia by the brook of death.]

After the always immitigable gloom of *Timon* and the sometimes malodorous exhalations of the three preceding plays, it is nothing less than "very heaven" to find and feel ourselves again in the midmost Paradise, the central Eden, of Shakespeare's divine discovery—of his last sweet living invention. Here again is air as pure blowing over fields as fragrant as where Dante saw Matilda or Milton saw Proserpine gathering each as deathless flowers. We still have here to disentwine or disentangle his own from the weeds of glorious and of other than glorious feature with which Fletcher has thought fit to interweave them; even in the close of the last scene of all we can say to a line, to a letter, where Shakespeare ends and Fletcher begins. That scene is opened by Shakespeare in his most majestic vein of meditative or moral verse, pointed and coloured as visual with him alone by direct and absolute aptitude to the immediate sentiment and situation of the speaker and of no man else: then either Fletcher strikes in for a moment with a touch of somewhat more Shakespearean tone than usual, or possibly we have a survival of some lines' length, not unretouched by Fletcher, from Shakespeare's first sketch for a conclusion of the somewhat calamitous and cumbrous underplot, which in any case was ultimately left for Fletcher to expand into such a shape and bring by such means to such an end as we may safely swear that Shakespeare would never have admitted: then with the entrance and ensuing narrative of Pirithous we have none but Shakespeare before us again, though it be Shakespeare undoubtedly in the rough, and not as he might have chosen to present himself after due revision, with rejection (we may well suppose) of this point and readjustment of that: then upon the arrival of the dying Arcite with his escort there follows a grievous little gap, a flaw but pitifully patched by Fletcher, whom we recognise at wellnigh his worst and weakest in Palamon's appeal to his kinsman for a last word, "if his heart, **his worthy, manly heart**" (an exact and typical example of Fletcher's tragically prosaic and prosaically tragic dash of incurable commonplace), "be yet unbroken," and in the flaccid and futile answer which fails so signally to supply the place of the most famous and pathetic passage in all the masterpiece of Chaucer; a passage to which even Shakespeare could have added but some depth and grandeur of his own giving, since neither he nor Dante's very self nor any other among the divinest of men could have done more or better than match it for tender and pure simplicity of words more "dearly sweet and bitter" than the bitterest or the sweetest of men's tears. Then, after the duly and properly conventional engagement on the parts of Palamon and Emilia respectively to devote the anniversary "to tears" and "to honour," the deeper note returns for one grand last time, grave at once and sudden and sweet as the full choral opening of an anthem: the note which none could ever catch of Shakespeare's very voice gives out the peculiar cadence that it alone can give in the modulated instinct of a solemn change or shifting of the metrical emphasis or *ictus* from one to the other of two repeated words:—

That nought could buy
Dear love, but loss of dear love!

That is a touch beyond the ear or the hand of Fletcher: a chord sounded from Apollo's own harp after a somewhat hoarse and reedy wheeze from the scrannel-pipe of a lesser player than Pan. Last of all, in words worthy to be the latest left of Shakespeare's, his great and gentle Theseus winds up the heavenly harmonies of his last beloved great poem.

And now, coming at length within the very circle of Shakespeare's culminant and crowning constellation, bathing my whole soul and spirit for the last and (if I live long enough) as surely for the first of many thousand times in the splendours of the planet whose glory is the light of his very love itself, standing even as Dante

> in the clear
> Amorous silence of the Swooning-sphere,

what shall I say of thanksgiving before the final feast of Shakespeare?

The grace must surely be short enough if it would at all be gracious. Even were Shakespeare's self alive again, or he now but fifteen years since gone home to Shakespeare, [Note 1: On the 17th of September, 1864] of whom Charles Lamb said well that none could have written his book about Shakespeare but either himself alone or else he of whom the book was written, yet could we not hope that either would have any new thing to tell us of the **Tempest,** the **Winters Tale,** and **Cymbeline.** And for ourselves, what else could we do but only ring changes on the word beautiful as Celia on the word wonderful in her laughing litany of love? or what better or what more can we do than in the deepest and most heartfelt sense of an old conventional phrase, thank God and Shakespeare? for how to praise either for such a gift of gifts we know not, knowing only and surely that none will know for ever.

True or false, and it would now seem something less than likely to be true, the fancy which assumed the last lines spoken by Prospero to be likewise the last words of the last completed work of Shakespeare was equally in either case at once natural and graceful. There is but one figure sweeter than Miranda's and sublimer than Prosperous in all the range of heaven on which the passion of our eyes could rest at parting. And from one point of view there is even a more heavenly quality perceptible in the light of this than of its two twin stars. In no nook or corner of the island as we leave it is any savour left or any memory lingering of any inexpiable evil. Alonzo is absolved; even Antonio and Sebastian have made no such ineffaceable mark on it by the presence of their pardoned crimes as is made by those which cost the life of Mamillius and the labours of Imogen. Poor Caliban is left in such comfort as may be allowed him by divine grace in the favourable aspect of Setebos; and his comrades go by us "reeling ripe" and "gilded" not by "grand liquor" only but also by the summer lightning of men's laughter: blown softly out of our sight, with a sound and a gust of music, by the breath of the song of Ariel.

The wild wind of the ***Winters Tale*** at its opening would seem to blow us back into a wintrier world indeed. And to the very end I must confess that I have in me so much of the spirit of Rachel weeping in Ramah as will not be comforted because Mamillius is not. It is well for those whose hearts are light enough, to take perfect comfort even in the substitution of his sister Perdita for the boy who died of "thoughts high for one so tender," Even the beautiful suggestion that Shakespeare as he wrote had in mind his own dead little son still fresh and living at his heart can hardly add more than a touch of additional tenderness to our perfect and piteous delight in him. And even in her daughter's embrace it seems hard if his mother should have utterly forgotten the little voice that had only time to tell her just eight words of that ghost story which neither she nor we were ever to hear ended. Any one but Shakespeare would have sought to make pathetic profit out of the child by the easy means of showing him if but once again as changed and stricken to the death for want of his mother and fear for her and hunger and thirst at his little high heart for the sight and touch of her: Shakespeare only could find a better way, a subtler and a deeper chord to strike, by giving us our last glimpse of him as he laughed and chattered with her "past enduring," to the shameful neglect of those ladies in the natural blueness of whose eyebrows as well as their noses he so stoutly declined to believe. And at the very end (as aforesaid) it may be that we remember him all the better because the father whose jealousy killed him and the mother for love of whom he died would seem to have forgotten the little brave sweet spirit with all its truth of love and tender sense of shame as perfectly and unpardonably as Shakespeare himself at the close of ***King Lear*** would seem to have forgotten one who never had forgotten Cordelia.

But yet—and here for once the phrase abhorred by Cleopatra does not "allay the good" but only the bad. "precedence"—if ever amends could be made for such unnatural show of seeming forgetfulness ("out on the seeming! I will write against it"—or would, had I not written enough already), the poet most assuredly has made such amends here. At the sunrise of Perdita beside Florizel it seems as if the snows of sixteen winters had melted all together into the splendour of one unutterable spring. They "smell April and May" in a sweeter sense than it could be said of "young Master Fenton" "nay, which is more," as his friend and champion Mistress Quickly might have added to mine host's commendatory remark, they speak all April and May; because April is in him as, naturally as May in her, by just so many years' difference before the Mayday of her birth as went to make up her dead brother's little lot of living breath, which in Beaumont's most lovely and Shakespeare-worthy phrase "was not a life; was but a piece of childhood thrown away." Nor can I be content to find no word of old affection for Autolycus, who lived, as we may not doubt, though but a hint or promise be vouchsafed us for all assurance that he lived by favour of his "good masters" once more to serve Prince Florizel and wear three-pile for as much of his time as it might please him to put on "robes" like theirs that were "gentlemen born," and had "been so any time these four hours." And yet another and a graver word must be given with all reverence to the "grave and good Paulina," whose glorious fire of godlike indignation was as warmth and cordial to the innermost heart while yet bruised and wrung for the yet fresh loss of Mamillius.

The time is wellnigh come now for me to consecrate in this book my good will if not good work to the threefold and thrice happy memory of the three who have written of Shakespeare as never man wrote, nor ever man may write again; to the everlasting praise and honour and glory of Charles Lamb, Samuel Taylor Coleridge, and Walter Savage Landor; "wishing," I hardly dare to say, "what I write may be read by their light." The play of plays, which is ***Cymbelin,*** remains alone to receive the last salute of all my love.

I think, as far as I can tell, I may say I have always loved this one beyond all other children of Shakespeare. The too literal egoism of this profession will not be attributed by any candid or even commonly honest reader to the violence of vanity so much more than comical as to make me suppose that such a record or assurance could in itself be matter of interest to any man: but simply to the real and simple reason, that I wish to show cause for my choice of this work to wind up with, beyond the mere chance of its position at the close of the chaotically inconsequent catalogue of contents affixed to the first edition. In this casualty—for no good thing can reasonably be ascribed to design on the part of the first editors—there would seem to be something more than usual of what we may call, if it so please us, a happy providence. It is certain that no studious arrangement could possibly have brought the book to a happier end. Here is depth enough with height enough of tragic beauty and passion, terror and love and pity, to approve the presence of the most tragic Master's hand; subtlety enough of sweet and bitter truth to attest the passage of the mightiest and wisest scholar or teacher in the school of the human spirit; beauty with delight enough and glory of life and grace of nature to proclaim the advent of the one omnipotent Maker among all who bear that name. Here above all is the most heavenly triad of human figures that ever even Shakespeare brought together; a diviner three, as it were a living god-garland of the noblest earth-born brothers and loveworthiest heaven-born sister, than the very givers of all grace and happiness to their Grecian worshippers of old time over long before. The passion of Posthumus is noble, and potent the poison of Iachimo; Cymbeline has enough for Shakespeare's present purpose of "the king-becoming graces"; but we think first and last of her who was "truest speaker" and those who "called her brother, when she was but their sister; she them brothers, when they were so indeed." The very crown and flower of all her father's daughters,—I do not speak here of her human father, but her divine—the woman above all Shakespeare's women is Imogen. As in Cleopatra we found the incarnate sex, the woman everlasting, so in Imogen we find half glorified already the immortal godhead of womanhood. I would fain have some honey in my words at parting—with Shakespeare never, but for ever with these notes on Shakespeare; and I am therefore something more than fain to close my book upon the name of the woman best beloved in all the world of song and all the tide of time; upon the name of Shakespeare's Imogen.

APPENDIX.

NOTE ON THE HISTORICAL PLAY OF KING EDWARD III.

THE epitaph of German criticism on Shakespeare was long since written by the unconscious hand which penned the following sentence; an inscription worthy of perpetual record on the registers of Gotham or in the daybook of the yet unstranded Ship of Fools.

"Thomas Lord Cromwell:—Sir John Oldcastle:—A Yorkshire Tragedy.—The three last pieces are not only unquestionably Shakespeare's, but in my opinion they deserve to be classed among his best and maturest works."

This memorable opinion is the verdict of the modest and judicious Herr von Schlegel: who had likewise in his day the condescension to inform our ignorance of the melancholy fact so strangely overlooked by the contemporaries of Christopher Marlowe, that "his verses are flowing, but without energy." Strange, but true; too strange, we may reasonably infer, not to be true. Only to German eyes has the treasure-house of English poetry ever disclosed a secret of this kind: to German ears alone has such discord or default been ever perceptible in its harmonies.

Now the facts with regard to this triad of plays are briefly these. ***Thomas Lord Cromwell*** is a piece of such utterly shapeless, spiritless, bodiless, soulless, senseless, helpless, worthless rubbish, that there is no known writer of Shakespeare's age to whom it could be ascribed without the infliction of an unwarrantable insult on that writer's memory. ***Sir John Oldcastle*** is the compound piecework of four minor playwrights, one of them afterwards and otherwise eminent as a poet—Munday, Drayton, Wilson, and Hathaway: a thin sample of poetic patchery cobbled up and stitched together so as to serve its hour for a season without falling to pieces at the first touch. The ***Yorkshire Tragedy*** is a coarse, crude, and vigorous impromptu, in which we possibly might almost think it possible that Shakespeare had a hand (or at least a finger), if we had any reason to suppose that during the last ten or twelve years of his life [Note 1: The once too celebrated crime which in this play was exhibited on the public stage with the forcible fidelity of a wellnigh brutal realism took actual place on the private stage of fact in the year 1604. Four years afterwards the play was published as Shakespeare's. Eight years more, and Shakespeare was with Æschylus] he was likely to have taken part in any such dramatic improvisation.

The example and the exposure of Schlegel's misadventures in this line have not sufficed to warn off minor blunderers from treading with emulous confidence "through forthrights and meanders" in the very muddiest of their precursor's traces. We may notice, for one example, the revival—or at least the discussion as of something worth serious notice—of a wellnigh still-born theory, first dropped in a modest corner of the critical world exactly a hundred and seventeen years ago. Its parent, notwithstanding this perhaps venial indiscretion, was apparently an honest and modest gentleman; and the play itself, which this ingenuous theorist was fain, with all diffidence, to try whether haply he might be permitted to foist on the apocryphal fatherhood of Shakespeare, is not without such minor merits as may excuse us for wasting a few minutes on examination of the theory which seeks to confer on it the factitious and artificial attraction of a spurious and adventitious interest.

"The Raigne of King Edward the third: As it hath bin sundrie times plaied about the Citie of London," was published in 1596, and ran through two or three anonymous editions before the date of the generation was out which first produced it. Having thus run to the end of its natural tether, it fell as naturally into the oblivion which has devoured, and has not again disgorged, so many a more precious production of its period. In 1760 it was reprinted in the "Prolusions" of Edward Capell, whose text is now before me. This editor was the first mortal to suggest that his newly unearthed treasure might possibly be a windfall from the topless tree of Shakespeare. Being, as I have said, a duly modest and an evidently honest man, he admits "with candour" that there is no jot or tittle of "external evidence" whatsoever to be alleged in support of this gratuitous attribution: but he submits, with some fair show of reason, that there is a certain "resemblance between the style of" Shakespeare's "earlier performances and of the work in question"; and without the slightest show of any reason whatever he appends to this humble and plausible plea the unspeakably unhappy assertion that at the time of its appearance "there was no known writer equal to such a play"; whereas at a moderate computation there were, I should say, on the authority of Henslowe's Diary, at least a dozen—and not improbably a score. In any case there was one then newly dead, too long before his time, whose memory stands even higher above the possible ascription of such a work than that of the adolescent Shakespeare's very self.

Of one point we may be sure, even where so much is unsure as we find it here: in the curt atheological phrase of the Persian Lucretius, "one thing is certain, and the rest is lies." The author of ***King Edward III.*** was a devout student and a humble follower of Christopher Marlowe, not yet wholly disengaged by that august and beneficent influence from all attraction towards the "jigging veins of rhyming mother-wits"; and fitter on the whole to follow this easier and earlier vein of writing, half lyrical in manner and half elegiac, than to brace upon his punier limbs the young giant's newly fashioned buskin of blank verse. The signs of this growing struggle, the traces of this incomplete emancipation, are perceptible throughout in the alternate prevalence of two conflicting and irreconcilable styles; which yet affords no evidence or suggestion of a double authorship. For the intelligence which moulds and informs the whole work, the spirit which pervades and imbues the general design, is of a piece, so to speak, throughout; a point imperceptible to the eye, a touchstone intangible by the finger, alike of a scholiast and a dunce.

Another test, no less unmistakable by the student and no less indiscernible to the sciolist, is this: that whatever may be the demerits of this play, they are due to no voluntary or involuntary carelessness or haste. Here is not the swift impatient journeywork of a rough and ready hand; here is no sign of such compulsory hurry in the discharge of a task something less than welcome, if not of an imposition something less than tolerable, as we may rationally believe ourselves able to trace in great part of Marlowe's work: in the latter half of ***The Jew of Malta,*** in the burlesque interludes of ***Doctor Faustus,*** and wellnigh throughout the whole scheme and course of ***The Massacre at Paris.*** Whatever in ***King Edward III.*** is mediocre or worse is evidently such as it is through no passionate or slovenly precipitation of handiwork, but through pure incompetence to do better. The blame of the failure, the shame of the shortcoming, cannot be laid to the account of any momentary excess or default in emotion, of passing exhaustion or excitement, of intermittent impulse and reaction; it is an indication of lifelong and irremediable impotence. And it is further to be noted that by far the least unsuccessful parts of the play are also by far the most unimportant The capacity of the author seems to shrink and swell alternately, to erect its plumes and deject them, to contract and to dilate the range and orbit of its flight in a steadily inverse degree to the proportionate interest of the subject or worth of the topic in hand. There could be no surer proof that it is neither the early nor the hasty work of a great or even a remarkable poet. It is the best that could be done at any time by a conscientious and studious workman of technically insufficient culture and of naturally limited means.

I would not, however, be supposed to undervalue the genuine and graceful ability of execution displayed by the author at his best. He could write at times very much after the earliest fashion of the adolescent Shakespeare; in other words, after the fashion of the day or hour, to which in some degree the greatest writer of that hour or that day cannot choose but conform at starting, and the smallest writer must needs conform for ever. By the rule which would attribute to Shakespeare every line written in his first manner which appeared during the first years of his poetic progress, it is hard to say what amount of bad verse or better, current during the rise and the reign of their several influences,—for this kind of echo or of copywork, consciously or unconsciously repercussive and reflective, begins with the very first audible sound of a man's voice in song, with the very first noticeable stroke of his hand in painting—it is hard to say what amount of tolerable or intolerable work might not or may not be assignable by scholiasts of the future to Byron or to Shelley, to Mr. Tennyson or to Mr. Browning. A time by this rule might come—but I am fain to think better of the Fates—when by comparison of detached words and collation of dismembered phrases the memory of Mr. Tennyson would be weighted and degraded by the ascription of whole volumes of pilfered and diluted verse now current—if not yet submerged—under the name or the pseudonym of the present Viceroy—or Vice-empress is it?—of India. But the obvious truth is this: the voice of Shakespeare's adolescence had as usual an echo in it of other men's notes: I can remember the name of but one poet whose voice from the beginning had none; who started with a style of his own, though he may have chosen to annex—"annex the wise it call"; ***convey*** is obsolete—to annex whole phrases or whole verses at need, for the use or the ease of an idle minute; and this name of course is Marlowe's. So starting, Shakespeare had yet (like all other and lesser poets born) some perceptible notes in his yet half boyish voice that were not borrowed; and these were at once caught up and re-echoed by such fellow-pupils with Shakespeare of the young Master of them all—such humbler and feebler disciples, or simpler sheep (shall we call them?) of the great "dead shepherd"—as the now indistinguishable author of ***King Edward III.***

In the first scene of the first act the impotent imitation of Marlowe is pitifully patent. Possibly there may also be an imitation of the still imitative style of Shakespeare, and the style may be more accurately definable as a copy of a copy—a study after the manner of Marlowe, not at second hand, but at third. In any case, being obviously too flat and feeble to show a touch of either godlike hand, this scene may be set aside at once to make way for the second.

The second scene is more animated, but low in style till we come to the outbreak of rhyme. In other words, the energetic or active part is at best passable—fluent and decent commonplace: but where the style turns un-dramatic and runs into mere elegiacs, a likeness becomes perceptible to the first elegiac style of Shakespeare. Witness these lines spoken by the King in contemplation of the Countess of Salisbury's beauty, while yet struggling against the nascent motions of a base love:—

Now in the sun alone it doth not lie
With light to take light from a mortal eye:
For here two day-stars that mine eyes would see
More than the sun steal mine own light from me.
Contemplative desire! desire to be
In contemplation that may master thee!

Decipit exemplar uitiis imitabile: if Shakespeare ever saw or heard these pretty lines, he should have felt the unconscious rebuke implied in such close and facile imitation of his own early elegiacs. As a serious mimicry of his first manner, a critical parody summing up in little space the sweet faults of his poetic nonage, with its barren overgrowth of unprofitable flowers,—bright point, soft metaphor, and sweet elaborate antithesis—this is as good of its kind as anything between Aristophanes and Horace Smith. Indeed, it may remind us of that parody on the soft, superfluous, flowery and frothy style of Agathon, which at the opening of the Thesmophoriazusæ cannot but make the youngest and most ignorant reader laugh, though the oldest and most learned has never set eyes on a line of the original verses which supplied the incarnate god of comic song with matter for such exquisite burlesque.

To the speech above cited the reply of the Countess is even gracefuller, and closer to the same general model of fanciful elegiac dialogue:—

> Let not thy presence, like the April sun,
> Flatter our earth, and suddenly be done:
> More happy do not make our outward wall
> Than thou wilt grace our inward house withal.
> Our house, my liege, is like a country swain,
> Whose habit rude, and manners blunt and plain,
> Presageth naught; yet inly beautified
> With bounty's riches, and fair hidden pride;
> For where the golden ore doth buried lie,
> The ground, undecked with nature's tapestry,
> Seems barren, sere, unfertile, fruitless, dry;
> And where the upper turf of earth doth boast

His pride, perfumes, [Note 1: Capell has altered this to "proud perfumes" marking the change in a note, with the scrupulous honesty which would seem to have usually distinguished him from more daring and more famous editors] and particoloured cost,

> Delve there, and find this issue and their pride
> To spring from ordure and corruption's side.

> But, to make up my all too long compare,
> These ragged walls no testimony are
> What is within; but, like a cloak, doth hide
> From weather's waste the under garnished pride.
> More gracious than my terms can let thee be,
> Entreat thyself to stay awhile with me.

Not only the exquisite grace of this charming last couplet, but the smooth sound strength, the fluency and clarity of the whole passage, may serve to show that the original suggestion of Capell, if (as I think) untenable, was not (we must admit) unpardonable. The very oversight perceptible to any eye and painful to any ear not sealed up by stepdame nature from all perception of pleasure or of pain derivable from good verse or bad—the reckless reiteration of the same rhyme with but one poor couplet intervening—suggests rather the oversight of an unfledged poet than the obtuseness of a full-grown poeticule or poetaster.

But of how many among the servile or semi-servile throng of imitators in every generation may not as much as this be said by tolerant or kindly judges! Among the herd of such diminutives as swarm after the heel or fawn upon the hand of Mr. Tennyson, more than one, more than two or three, have come as close as his poor little viceregal or vice-imperial parasite to the very touch and action of the master's hand which feeds them unawares from his platter as they fawn; as close as this nameless and short-winded satellite to the gesture and the stroke of Shakespeare's. For this also must be noted; that the resemblance here is but of stray words, of single lines, of separable passages. The whole tone of the text, the whole build of the play, the whole scheme of the poem, is far enough from any such resemblance. The structure, the composition, is feeble, incongruous, inadequate, effete. Any student will remark at a first glance what a short-breathed runner, what a broken-winded athlete in the lists of tragic verse, is the indiscoverable author of this play.

There is another point which the Neo-Shakespearean synagogue will by no man be expected to appreciate; for to apprehend it requires some knowledge and some understanding of the poetry of the Shakespearean age—so surely we now should call it, rather than Elizabethan or Jacobean, for the sake of verbal convenience, if not for the sake of literary decency; and such knowledge or understanding no sane man will expect to find in any such quarter. Even in the broad coarse comedy of the period we find here and there the same sweet and simple echoes of the very cradle-song (so to call it) of our drama: so like Shakespeare, they might say who knew nothing of Shakespeare's fellows, that we cannot choose but recognise his hand. Here as always first in the field—the genuine and golden harvest-field of Shakespearean criticism, Charles Lamb has cited a passage from **Green's Tu Quoque**—a comedy miserably misprinted in Dodsley's Old Plays—on which he observes that "this is so like Shakespeare, that we seem to remember it," being as it is a girl's gentle lamentation over the selfish, exacting, suspicious and trustless love of man, as contrasted with the swift simple surrender of a woman's love at the first heartfelt appeal to her pity—"we seem to remember it," says Lamb, as a speech of Desdemona uttered on a first perception or suspicion of jealousy or alienation in Othello. This lovely passage, if I dare say so in contravention to the authority of Lamb, is indeed as like the manner of Shakespeare as it can be—to eyes ignorant of what his fellows can do; but it is not like the manner of the Shakespeare who wrote **Othello.** This, however, is beside the question. It is very like the Shakespeare who wrote the Comedy of Errors—Love's Labour's Lost—Romeo and Juliet. *It is so like that had are fallen upon it in any of these play s it would long since have been a household word in all men's mouths for sweetness, truth, simplicity, perfect and instinctive accuracy of touch. It is very much liker the first manner of Shakespeare than any passage in* King Edward III. *And no Sham Shakespearean critic that I know of has yet assigned to the hapless object of his howling homage the authorship of* Green's Tu Quoque.

Returning to our text, we find in the short speech of the King with which the first act is wound up yet another couplet which has the very ring in it of Shakespeare's early notes—the catch at words rather than play on words which his tripping tongue in youth could never resist:

Countess, albeit my business urgeth me,

It shall attend while I attend on thee.

And with this pretty little instance of courtly and courteous euphuism we pass from the first to the second and most important act in the play.

Any reader well versed in the text of Shakespeare, and ill versed in the work of his early rivals and his later pupils, might surely be forgiven if on a first reading of the speech with which this act opens he should cry out with Capell that here at least was the unformed hand of the Master perceptible and verifiable indeed. The writer, he might say, has the very glance of his eye, the very trick of his gait, the very note of his accent. But on getting a little more knowledge, such a reader will find the use of it in the perception to which he will have attained that in his early plays, as in his two early poems, the style of Shakespeare was not for the most part distinctively his own. It was that of a crew, a knot of young writers, among whom he found at once both leaders and followers to be guided and to guide. A mere glance into the rich lyric literature of the period will suffice to show the dullest eye and teach the densest ear how nearly innumerable were the Englishmen of Elizabeth's time who could sing in the courtly or pastoral key of the season, each man of them a few notes of his own, simple or fantastic, but all sweet, clear, genuine of their kind:—

Facies non omnibus una,
Nec diversa tamen:

and yet so close is the generic likeness between flower and flower of the same lyrical garden that the first half of the quotation seems but half applicable here. In Bird's, Morley's, Dowland's collections of music with the words appended—in such jewelled volumes as ***England's Helicon*** and ***Davison's Poetical Rhapsody***—their name is Legion, their numbers are numberless. You cannot call them imitators, this man of that, or all of any; they were all of one school, but it was a school without a master or a head. And even so it was with the earliest sect or gathering of dramatic writers in England. Marlowe alone stood apart and above them all—the young Shakespeare among the rest; but among these we cannot county, we cannot guess, how many were wellnigh as competent as he to continue the fluent rhyme, to prolong the facile echo, of Greene and Peele, their first and most famous leaders.

No more docile or capable pupil could have been desired by any master in any art than the author of **Davia and Bethsabe** has found in the writer of this second act.

He has indeed surpassed his model, if not in grace and sweetness, yet in taste or tact of expression, in continuity and equality of style. Vigour is not the principal note of his manner, but compared with the soft effusive ebullience of his master's we may fairly call it vigorous and condensed. But all this merit or demerit is matter of mere language only. The poet—a very pretty poet in his way, and doubtless capable of gracious work enough in the idyllic or elegiac line of business—shows about as much capacity to grasp and handle the fine intimacies of character and the large issues of circumstance to any tragic or dramatic purpose, as might be expected from an idyllic or elegiac poet who should suddenly assume the buskin of tragedy. Let us suppose that Moschus, for example, on the strength of having written a sweeter elegy than ever before was chanted over the untimely grave of a friend and fellow-singer, had said within himself, "Go to, I will be Sophocles"; can we imagine that the tragic result would have been other than tragical indeed for the credit of his gentle name, and comical indeed for all who might have envied the mild and modest excellence which fashion or hypocrisy might for years have induced them to besprinkle with the froth and slaver of their promiscuous and pointless adulation?

As the play is not more generally known than it deserves to be,—or perhaps we may say it is somewhat less known, though its claim to general notice is faint indeed compared with that of many a poem of its age familar only to special students in our own—I will transcribe a few passages to show how far the writer could reach at his best; leaving for others to indicate how far short of that not inaccessible point he is too generally content to fall and to remain.

The opening speech is spoken by one Lodowick, a parasite of the King's; who would appear, like François Villon under the roof of his Fat Madge, to have succeeded in reconciling the professional duties—may I not say, the generally discordant and discrepant offices?—of a poet and a pimp.

> I might perceive his eye in her eye lost,
> His ear to drink her sweet tongue's utterance;
> And changing passion, like inconstant clouds,
> That, rackt upon the carriage of the winds,
> Increase, and die, in his disturbed cheeks.
> Lo, when she blushed, even then did he look pale;
> As if her cheeks by some enchanted power
> Attracted had the cherry blood from his: [Note 1: The feeble archaic inversion in this line is one among many small signs which all together suffice, if not to throw back the date of this play to the years immediately preceding the advent of Marlowe or the full influence of his genius and example, yet certainly to mark it as an instance of survival from that period of incomposite and inadequate workmanship in verse].
> Anon, with reverent fear when she grew pale,
> His cheeks put on their scarlet ornaments;
> But no more like her oriental red
> Than brick to coral, or live things to dead [Note 2: Or than this play to a genuine work of Shakespeare's. "Brick to coral"—these three words describe exactly the difference in tone and shade of literary colour.]
> Why did he then thus counterfeit her looks?
> If she did blush, 'twas tender modest shame,
> Being in the sacred presence of a king;
> If he did blush, 'twas red immodest shame
>
> To vail his eyes amiss, being a king;
> If she looked pale, 'twas silly woman's fear
> To bear herself in presence of a king;
> If he looked pale, it was with guilty fear
> To dote amiss, being a mighty king.

This is better than the insufferable style of **Locrine,** which is in great part made up of such rhymeless couplets, each tagged with an empty verbal antithesis; but taken as a sample of dramatic writing, it is but just better than what is utterly intolerable. Dogberry has defined it exactly; it is most tolerable—and not to be endured.

The following speech of King Edward is in that better style of which the author's two chief models were not at their best incapable for awhile under the influence and guidance (we may suppose) of their friend Marlowe.

> She is grown more fairer far since I came hither;
> Her voice more silver every word than other,
> Her wit more fluent. What a strange discourse
> Unfolded she of David and his Scots!
> ***Even thus,*** quoth she, ***he spake***—and then spake broad,
> With epithets and accents of the Scot;
> But somewhat better than the Scot could speak:
> ***And thus,*** quoth she—and answered then herself;
> For who could speak like her? but she herself
> Breathes from the wall an angel's note from heaven
> Of sweet defiance to her barbarous foes.
> When she would talk of peace, methinks her tongue
> Commanded war to prison; [Note 1: Here for the first time we come upon a verse not unworthy of Marlowe himself—a verse in spirit as in cadence recalling the deep oceanic reverberations of his "mighty line," profound and just and simple and single as a note of the music of the sea. But it would be hard if a devout and studious disciple were never to catch one passing tone of his master's habitual accent.—It may be worth while to observe that we find here the same modulation of verse—common enough since then, but new to the patient auditors of ***Gorboduc*** and ***Locrine***—which we find in the finest passage of Marlowe's imperfect play of ***Dido,*** completed by Nash after the young Master's untimely death.

> Why star'st thou in my face? If thou wilt stay,
> Leap in my arms: mine arms are open wide:

If not—turn from me, and I'll turn from thee;
For though thou hast the power to say farewell,
I have not power to stay thee.

But we may look long in vain for the like of this passage, taken from the crudest and feeblest work of Marlowe, in the wide and wordy expanse of *King Edward III.*] when of war,
It wakened Cæsar from his Roman grave
To hear war beautified by her discourse.
Wisdom is foolishness, but in her tongue;
Beauty a slander, but in her fair face;
There is no summer but in her cheerful looks,
Nor frosty winter but in her disdain.
I cannot blame the Scots that did besiege her,
For she is all the treasure of our land;
But call them cowards that they ran away,
Having so rich and fair a cause to stay.

But if for a moment we may fancy that here and there we have caught such an echo of Marlowe as may have fallen from the lips of Shakespeare in his salad days, in his period of poetic pupilage, we have but a very little way to go forward before we come upon indisputable proof that the pupil was one of feebler hand and fainter voice than Shakespeare. Let us take the passage on poetry, beginning—

Now, Lodowick, invocate [Note 1: A pre-Shakespearean word of single occurrence in a single play of Shakespeare's, and proper to the academic school of playwrights.] some golden Muse
To bring thee hither an enchanted pen;

and so forth. No scholar in English poetry but will recognise at once the flat and futile imitation of Marlowe; not of his great general style alone, but of one special and transcendant passage which can never be too often quoted.

> If all the pens that ever poets held
> Had fed the feeling of their masters' thoughts,
> And every sweetness that inspired their hearts,
> Their minds, and muses on admired themes;
> If all the heavenly quintessence they still
> From their immortal flowers of poesy,
> Wherein, as in a mirror, we perceive
> The highest reaches of a human wit;
> If these had made one poem's period,
> And all combined in beauty's worthiness,
> Yet should there hover in their restless heads
> One thought, one grace, one wonder, at the least,
> Which into words no virtue can digest. [Note 1: ***The First Part of Tamburlaine the Great,*** Act v. Sc. ii.]

Infinite as is the distance between the long roll of these mighty lines and the thin tinkle of their feeble imitator's, yet we cannot choose but catch the ineffectual note of a would-be echo in the speech of the King to his parasite—

> For so much moving hath a poet's pen, etc., etc.

It is really not worth while to transcribe the poor meagre versicles at length: but a glance at the text will show how much fitter was their author to continue the tradition of Peele than to emulate the innovations of Marlowe. In the speeches that follow there is much pretty verbiage after the general manner of Elizabethan sonnetteers, touched here and there with something of a higher tone; but the whole scene drags, flags, halts onward at such a languid rate, that to pick out all the prettiest lines by way of sample would give a favourable impression but too likely to be reversed on further and fuller acquaintance.

> Forget not to set down, how passionate,
> How heart-sick, and how full of languishment,
> Her beauty makes me . . . . .

> Write on, while I peruse her in my thoughts.
> Her voice to music, or the nightingale:
> To music every summer-leaping swain
> Compares his sunburnt lover when she speaks;
> And why should I speak of the nightingale?
> The nightingale sings of adulterate wrong;
> And that, compared, is too satirical:
> For sin, though sin, would not be so esteemed;
> But rather virtue sin, sin virtue deemed.
> Her hair, far softer than the silkworm's twist,
> Like as a flattering glass, doth make more fair
> The yellow amber:—***Like a flattering glass***
> Comes in too soon; for, writing of her eyes,
> I'll say that like a glass they catch the sun,
> And thence the hot reflection doth rebound
> Against my breast, and burns the heart within.
> Ah, what a world of descant makes my soul
> Upon this voluntary ground of love!

Pretty enough, very pretty! but" exactly as like and as near the style of Shakespeare's early plays as is the style of Constable's sonnets to that of Shakespeare's. Unless we are to assign to the Master every unaccredited song, sonnet, elegy, tragedy, comedy, and farce of his period, which bears the same marks of the same date—a date, like our own, of too prolific and imitative production—as we find inscribed on the greater part of his own early work; unless we are to carry even as far as this the audacity and arrogance of our sciolism, we must somewhere make a halt—and it must be on the near side of such an attribution as that of ***King Edward III.*** to the hand of Shakespeare.

With the disappearance of the poetic pimp and the entrance of the unsuspecting Countess, the style rises yet again—and really, this time, much to the author's credit It would need a very fine touch from a very powerful hand to improve on the delicacy and dexterity of the prelude or overture to the King's avowal of adulterous love. But when all is said, though very delicate and very dexterous, it is not forcible work: I do not mean by forcible the same as violent, spasmodic, emphatic beyond the modesty of nature; a poet is of course only to be commended, and that heartily, for keeping within this bound; but he is not to be commended for coming short of it. This whole scene is full of mild and temperate beauty, of fanciful yet earnest simplicity; but the note of it, the expression, the dominant key of the style, is less appropriate to the utterance of a deep and deadly passion than—at the utmost—of what modern tongues might call a strong and rather dangerous flirtation. Passion, so to speak, is quite out of this writer's call; the depths and heights of manly as of womanly emotion are alike beyond his reach.

> Thought and affliction, passion, hell itself,
> He turns to favour and to prettiness.

"To favour and to prettiness"; the definition of his utmost merit and demerit, his final achievement and shortcoming, is here complete and exact. Witness the sweet quiet example of idyllic work which I extract from a scene beginning in the regular amœbæan style of ancient pastoral.

> *Edward.* Thou hear'st me say that I do dote on thee.
> *Countess.* If on my beauty, take it if thou canst;
> Though little, I do prize it ten times less:
> If on my virtue, take it if thou canst;
> For virtue's store by giving doth augment:
> Be it on what it will that I can give
> And thou canst take away, inherit it.
> *Edward.* It is thy beauty that I would enjoy.
> *Countess.* O, were it painted, I would wipe it off,
> And dispossess myself to give it thee:
> But, sovereign, it is soldered to my life;
> Take one and both; for like an humble shadow
> It haunts the sunshine of my summer's life.
> *Edward.* But thou mayst lend it me to sport withal.

Countess. As easy may my intellectual soul
Be lent away, and yet my body live,
As lend my body, palace to my soul,
Away from her, and yet retain my soul.
My body is her bower, her court, her abbey,
And she an angel, pure, divine, unspotted;
If I should lend her house, my lord, to thee,
I kill my poor soul, and my poor soul me.

Once more, this last couplet is very much in the style of Shakespeare's sonnets; nor is it wholly unlike even the dramatic style of Shakespeare in his youth—and some dozen other poets or poeticules of the time. But throughout this part of the play the recurrence of a faint and intermittent resemblance to Shakespeare is more frequently noticeable than elsewhere. [Note 1: It may be worth a remark that the word ***power*** is constantly used as a dissyllable another note of archaic debility or insufficiency in metre.] A student of imperfect memory but not of defective intuition might pardonably assign such couplets, on hearing them cited, to the master-hand itself; but such a student would be likelier to refer them to the sonnetteer than to the dramatist And a casual likeness to the style of Shakespeare's sonnets is not exactly sufficient evidence to warrant such an otherwise unwarrantable addition or appendage to the list of Shakespeare's plays.

A little further on we come upon the first and last passage which does actually recall by its wording a famous instance of the full and ripened style of Shakespeare.

He that doth clip or counterfeit your stamp
Shall die, my lord: and will your sacred self
Commit high treason 'gainst the King of heaven,
To stamp his image in forbidden metal,
Forgetting your allegiance and your oath?
In violating marriage' sacred law
You break a greater honour than yourself;

> To be a king is of a younger house
> Than to be married: your progenitor,
> Sole reigning Adam on the universe,
> By God was honoured for a married man,
> But not by him anointed for a king.

Every possible, reader, I suppose, will at once bethink himself of the famous passage in *Measure for Measure* which here may seem to be faintly prefigured:

> It were as good
> To pardon him that hath from nature stolen
> A man already made, as to remit
> Their saucy sweetness, that do coin heaven's image
> In stamps that are forbid:

and the very difference of style is not wider than the gulf which gapes between the first style of Shakespeare and the last. But men of Shakespeare's stamp, I venture to think, do not thus repeat themselves. The echo of the passage in *A Midsummer Night's Dream,* describing the girlish friendship of Hermia and Helena, which we find in the first act of *The Two Noble Kinsmen,* describing the like girlish friendship of Emilia and Flavina, is an echo of another sort Both, I need hardly say, are unquestionably Shakespeare's; but the fashion in which the matured poet retouches and completes the sketch of his earlier years—composes an oil painting, as it were, from the hints and suggestions of a water-colour sketch long since designed and long since half forgotten—is essentially different from the mere verbal and literal trick of repetition which sciolists might think to detect in the present instance. Again we must needs fall back on the inevitable and indefinable test of style; a test which could be of no avail if we were foolish enough to appeal to scholiasts and their attendant dunces, but which should be of some avail if we appeal to experts and their attentive scholars; and by this test we can but remark that neither the passage in *A Midsummer Night's Dream* nor the corresponsive passage in *The Two Noble Kinsmen* could have been written by any hand known to us but Shakespeare's; whereas the passage in *King Edward III* might as certainly have been written by any one out of a dozen poets then living as the answering passage in *Measure for Measure* could assuredly have been written by Shakespeare alone.

As on a first reading of the *Hippolytus* of Euripides we feel that, for all the grace and freshness and lyric charm of its opening scenes, the claim of the poem to our ultimate approval or disapproval must needs depend on the success or failure of the first interview between Theseus and his calumniated son; and as on finding that scene to be feeble and futile and prosaic and verbose we feel that the poet who had a woman's spite against women has here effectually and finally shown himself powerless to handle the simplest elements of masculine passion, of manly character and instinct; so in this less important case we feel that the writer, having ventured on such a subject as the compulsory temptation of a daughter by a father, who has been entrapped into so shameful an undertaking through the treacherous exaction of an equivocal promise unwarily confirmed by an inconsiderate oath, must be judged by the result of his own enterprise; must fall or stand as a poet by its failure or success. And his failure is only not complete; he is but just redeemed from utter discomfiture by the fluency and simplicity of his equable but inadequate style. Here as before we find plentiful examples of the gracefully conventional tone current among the lesser writers of the hour.

> *Warwick.* How shall I enter on this graceless errand?
> I must not call her child; for where's the father
> That will in such a suit seduce his child?
> Then, *Wife of Salisbury*—shall I so begin?
> No, he's my friend; and where is found the friend
> That will do friendship such endamagement? [Note 1: Yet another essentially non-Shakespearean word, though doubtless once used by Shakespeare; this time a most ungraceful Gallicism.]—
> Neither my daughter, nor my dear friend's wife,
> I am not Warwick, as thou think'st I am,
> But an attorney from the court of hell;
> That thus have housed my spirit in his form
> To do a message to thee from the king.

This beginning is fair enough, if not specially fruitful in promise; but the verses following are of the flattest order of commonplace. Hay and grass and the spear of Achilles—of which tradition

> the moral is,
> What mighty men misdo, they can amend—

these are the fresh and original types on which our little poet is compelled to fall back for support and illustration to a scene so full of terrible suggestion and pathetic possibility.

> The king will in his glory hide thy shame;
> And those that gaze on him to find out thee
> Will lose their eyesight, looking on the sun.
> What can one drop of poison harm the sea,
> Whose hugy vastures can digest the ill
> And make it lose its operation?

And so forth, and so forth; **ad libitum** if not **ad nauseam.** Let us take but one or two more instances of the better sort.

> **Countess.** Unnatural besiege! Woe me unhappy,
> To have escaped the danger of my foes,
> And to be ten times worse invir'd by friends!

(Here we come upon two more words unknown to Shakespeare; [Note 1: It may obviate any chance of mistake if I observe that here as elsewhere, when I mention the name that is above every name in English literature, I refer to the old Shakespeare, and not to "the new Shakspere"; a **novus homo** with whom I have no acquaintance, and with whom (if we may judge of a great—or a little—unknown after the appearance and the bearing of those who select him as a social sponsor for themselves and their literary catechumens) I can most sincerely assert that I desire to have none.] ***besiege,*** as a noun substantive, and ***invired*** for ***environed.***)

> Hath he no means to stain my honest blood
> But to corrupt the author of my blood
> To be his scandalous and vile soliciter?
> No marvel though the branches be infected,
> When poison hath encompassed the roots;
> No marvel though the leprous infant die,
> When the stern dam envenometh the dug.
> Why then, give sin a passport to offend,
> And youth the dangerous rein of liberty;
> Blot out the strict forbidding of the law;
> And cancel every canon that prescribes
> A shame for shame or penance for offence.
> No, let me die, if his too boisterous will
> Will have it so, before I will consent
> To be an actor in his graceless lust.
> ***Warwick.*** Why, now thou speak'st as
> I would have thee speak;
> And mark how I unsay my words again.
> An honourable grave is more esteemed
> Than the polluted closet of a king;
> The greater man, the greater is the thing,
> Be it good or bad, that he shall undertake;
> An unreputed mote, flying in the sun,
> Presents a greater substance than it is;
> The freshest summer's day doth soonest taint
>
> The loathed carrion that it seems to kiss:
> Deep are the blows made with a mighty axe;
> That sin doth ten times aggravate itself
> That is committed in holy place;
> An evil deed, done by authority,

  Is sin, and subornation: Deck an ape
In tissue, and the beauty of the robe
Adds bat the greater scorn onto the beast.

(Here are four passably good lines, which vaguely remind the reader of something better read elsewhere; a common case enough with the more tolerable work of small imative poets.)

  A spacious field of reasons could I urge
Between his glory, daughter, and thy shame:
That poison shows worst in a golden cup;
Dark night seems darker by the lightning flash;
Lilies that fester smell far worse than weeds;
And very glory that inclines to sin,
The shame is treble by the opposite.
So leave I, with my blessing in thy bosom;
Which then convert to a most heavy curse,
When thou convert'st from honour's golden name
To the black faction of bed-blotting shame! [*Exit*
 Countess. I'll follow thee:—And when my mind turns NO, My body sink my soul in endless woe! [*Exit*

  So much for the central and crowning scene, the test, the climax, the hinge on which the first part of this play turns; and seems to me, in turning, to emit but a feeble and rusty squeak. No probable reader will need to be reminded that the line which I have perhaps unnecessarily italicised appears also as the last verse in the ninety-fourth of those "sugared sonnets" which we know were in circulation about the time of this play's first appearance among Shakespeare's "private friends"; in other words, which enjoyed such a kind of public privacy or private publicity as one or two among the most eminent English poets of our own day have occasionally chosen for some part of their work, to screen it for awhile as under the shelter and the shade of crepuscular laurels, till ripe for the sunshine or the storm of public judgment In the present case, this debatable verse looks to me more like a loan or maybe a theft from Shakespeare's private store of undramatic poetry than a misapplication by its own author to dramatic purposes of a line too apt and exquisite to endure without injury the transference from its original setting.

The scene ensuing winds up the first part of this composite (or rather, in one sense of the word, incomposite) poem. It may, on the whole, be classed as something more than passably good: it is elegant, lively, even spirited in style; showing at all events a marked advance upon the scene which I have already stigmatised as a failure—that which attempts to render the interview between Warwick and the King. It is hardly, however, I should say, above the highest reach of Greene or Peele at the smoothest and straightest of his flight. At its opening, indeed, we come upon a line which inevitably recalls one of the finest touches in a much later and deservedly more popular historical drama. On being informed by Derby that

> The king is in his closet, malcontent,
> For what I know not, but he gave in charge,
> Till after dinner, none should interrupt him;
> The Countess Salisbury, and her father Warwick,
> Artois, and all, look underneath the brows;

on receiving, I say, this ominous intimation, the prompt and statesmanlike sagacity of Audley leads him at once as by intuition to the inference thus eloquently expressed n a strain of thrilling and exalted poetry;

> Undoubtedly, then something is amiss.

Who can read this without a reminiscence of Sir Christopher Hatton's characteristically cautious conclusion at sight of the military preparations arrayed against the immediate advent of the Armada?

> I cannot but surmise—forgive, my friend,
> If the conjecture's rash—I cannot but
> Surmise the state some danger apprehends!

With the entrance of the King the tone of this scene naturally rises—"in good time," as most readers will say. His brief interview with the two nobles has at least the merit of ease and animation.

Derby. Befall my sovereign all my sovereign's wish!
Edward. Ah, that thou wert a witch, to make it so!
Derby. The emperor greeteth you.
Edward. Would it were the countess!
Derby. And hath accorded to your highness' suit.
Edward. Thou liest, she hath not: But I would she had!
Audley. All love and duty to my lord the king!
Edward. **Well, all but one is none:**—What news with you?
Audley. I have, my liege, levied those horse and foot,
According to jour charge, and brought them hither.

Edward. Then let those foot trudge hence upon those horse
According to their discharge, and begone.—
Derby, I'll look upon the countess' mind
Anon.
Derby. The countess' mind, my liege?
Edward. I mean, the emperor;—Leave me alone.
Audley. What's in his mind?
Derby. Let's leave him to his humour.
[*Exeunt DERBY and AUDLEY*
Edward. Thus from the heart's abundance speaks the tongue Countess for emperor: And indeed, why not?
She is as *imperator* over me;
And I to her
Am as a kneeling vassal, that observes
The pleasure or displeasure of her eye.

In this little scene there is perhaps on the whole more general likeness to Shakespeare's earliest manner than we can trace in any other passage of the play. But how much of Shakespeare's earliest manner may be accounted the special and exclusive property of Shakespeare?

After this dismissal of the two nobles, the pimping poeticule, Villon manqué or (whom shall we call him?) réussi, reappears with a message to Cæsar (as the King is pleased to style himself) from "the more than Cleopatra's match "(as he designates the Countess), to intimate that "ere night she will resolve his majesty." Hereupon an unseasonable "drum within" provokes Edward to the following remonstrance:

What drum is this, that thunders forth this march,
To start the tender Cupid in my bosom?
Poor sheepskin, how it brawls with him that beateth it!
Go, break the thundering parchment bottom out,
And I will teach it to conduct sweet lines

("That's bad; ***conduct sweet lines*** is bad.")

Unto the bosom of a heavenly nymph:
For I will use it as my writing paper;
And so reduce him, from a scolding drum,
To be the herald, and dear counsel-bearer,
Betwixt a goddess and a mighty king.
Go, bid the drummer learn to touch the lute,
Or hang him in the braces of his drum;
For now we think it an uncivil thing
To trouble heaven with such harsh resounds.
Away!   [***Exit*** LODOWICK.
The quarrel that I have requires no arms
But these of mine; and these shall meet my foe
In a deep march of penetrable groans;
My eyes shall be my arrows; and my sighs

Shall serve me as the vantage of the wind
To whirl away my sweet'st [Note 1: Surely, for **sweet'st** we should read **swift'st**] artillery:
Ah, but, alas, she wins the sun of me,
For that is she herself; and thence it comes
That poets term the wanton warrior blind;
But love hath eyes as judgment to his steps,
Till too much lovèd glory dazzles them.

Hereupon Lodowick introduces the Black Prince (that is to be), and "retires to the door." The following sceneens well, with a tone of frank and direct simplicity.

Edward. I see the boy. O, how his mother's face,
Moulded in his, corrects my strayed desire,
And rates my heart, and chides my thievish eye;
Who, being rich enough in seeing her,
Yet seeks elsewhere: and basest theft is that
Which cannot check itself on poverty.—
Now, boy, what news?
Prince. I have assembled, my dear lord and father,
The choicest buds of all our English blood,
For our affairs in France; and here we come
To take direction from your majesty.
Edward. Still do I see in him delineate
His mother's visage; those his eyes are hers,
Who, looking wistly [Note 1: This word occurs but once in Shakespeare's plays—] And speaking it, he wistly looked on me;

(*King Richard II.* Act v. Sc. 4.) and in such a case, as in the previous instances of the words *invocate* and *endamagement,* a mere can carry no weight of evidence with it worth any student's consideration] on me, made me blush;
For faults against themselves give evidence:
Lust is a fire; and men, like lanterns, show

Light lust within themselves even through themselves.
Away, loose silks of wavering vanity!
Shall the large limit of fair Brittany [Note 2: This form is used four times by Shakespeare as the equivalent of Bretagne; once only, in one of his latest plays, as a synonym for Britain.]
By me be overthrown? and shall I not
Master this little mansion of myself?
Give me an armour of eternal steel;
I go to conquer kings. And shall I then
Subdue myself, and be my enemy's friend?
It must not be.—Come, boy, forward, advance!
Let's with our colours sweep the air of France.

Here Lodowick announces the approach of the Countess "with a smiling cheer."

Edward. Why, there it goes! that very smile of hers
Hath ransomed captive France; and set the king,
The dauphin, and the peers, at liberty.—
Go, leave me, Ned, and revel with thy friends. [*Exit* PRINCE.
Thy mother is but black; and thou, like her,
Dost put into my mind how foul she is.
Go, fetch the countess hither in thy hand,
And let her chase away these winter clouds;
For she gives beauty both to heaven and earth.
[*Exit* LODOWICK.

The sin is more, to hack and hew poor men,
Than to embrace in an unlawful bed
The register of all rarieties [Note 1: Another word indiscoverable in any genuine verse of Shakespeare's, though not (I believe) unused on occasion by some among the poets contemporary with his earlier years.]
Since leathern Adam till this youngest hour.

Re-enter LODOWICK *with the* COUNTESS.

Go, Lodowick, put thy hand into my purse,
Play, spend, give, riot, waste; do what thou wilt,
So thou wilt hence awhile, and leave me here. [*Exit* LODOWICK.

Having already, out of a desire and determination to do no possible injustice to the actual merits of this play in the eyes of any reader who might never have gone over the text on which I had to comment, exceeded in no small degree the limits I had intended to impose upon my task in the way of citation, I shall not give so full a transcript from the next and last scene between the Countess and the King.

Edward. Now, my soul's playfellow! art thou come
To speak the more than heavenly word of yea
To my objection in thy beauteous love?

(Again, this singular use of the word *objection* in the sense of offer or proposal has no parallel in the plays of Shakespeare.)

Countess. My father on his blessing hath commanded—
Edward. That thou shalt yield to me.
Countess. Ay, dear my liege, your due.
Edward. And that, my dearest love, can be no less
Than right for right, and render [Note 2: This word was perhaps unnecessarily altered by our good Capell to "tender."] love for love.
Countess. Than wrong for wrong, and endless hate for hate.
But, sith I see your majesty so bent,
That my unwillingness, my husband's love,
Your high estate, nor no respect respected,
Can be my help, but that your mightiness
Will overbear and awe these dear regards,
I bind my discontent to my content,

And what I would not I'll compel I will;
Provided that yourself remove those lets
That stand between your highness' love and mine.
Edward. Name them, fair countess, and by heaven I will.
Countess. It is their lives that stand between our love
That I would have choked up, my sovereign.
Edward. Whose lives, my lady?
Countess.   My thrice loving liege,
Your queen, and Salisbury my wedded husband;
Who living have that title in our love
That we can not bestow but by their death.
Edward. Thy opposition [Note 1: Yet another and a singular misuse of a word never so used or misused by Shakespeare] is beyond our law.
Countess. So is your desire: If the law [Note 2: Qu. Why, so is your desire: If that the law, etc.?]
Can hinder you to execute the one,
Let it forbid you to attempt the other:
I cannot think you love me as you say
Unless you do make good what you have sworn.
Edward. No more: thy husband and the queen shall die.
Fairer thou art by far than Hero was;
Beardless Leander not so strong as I:
He sworn an easy current for his love;

But I will, through a helly spout of blood, [Note 3: **Sic.** I should once have thought it impossible that any mortal ear could endure the shock of this unspeakable and incomparable verse, and find in the passage which contains it an echo or a trace of the "music, wit, and oracle" of Shakespeare. But in those days I had yet to learn what manner of ears are pricked up to listen "when rank Thersites opes his mastiff jaws" in criticism of Homer or of Shakespeare. In a corner of the preface to an edition of "Shakspere" which bears on its title-page the name (correctly spelt) of Queen Victoria's youngest son prefixed to the name I have just transcribed, a small pellet of dry dirt was flung upwards at me from behind by the "able editor" thus irritably impatient to figure in public as the volunteer valet or literary lackey of Prince

Leopold. Hence I gathered the edifying assurance that this aspirant to the honours of literature in livery had been reminded of my humbler attempts in literature without a livery by the congenial music of certain four-footed fellow-critics and fellow-lodgers of his own in the neighbourhood of Hampstead Heath. Especially and most naturally had their native woodnotes wild recalled to the listening biped (whom partial nature had so far distinguished from the herd) the deep astonishment and the due disgust with which he had discovered the unintelligible fact that to men so ignorant of music or the laws of music in verse as my presumptuous and pitiable self the test of metrical harmony lay not in an appeal to the fingers but only in an appeal to the ear—"the ear which he" (that is, which the present writer) "makes so much of—AND WHICH SHOULD BE LONG TO MEASURE SHAKSPERE." Here then the great Sham Shakespearean secret is out at last. Had I but known in time my lifelong error in thinking that a capacity to estimate the refinements of word-music was not to be gauged by length of ear, by hairiness of ear, or by thickness of ear, but by delicacy of ear alone, I should as soon have thought of measuring my own poor human organs against those of the patriarch or leader of the herd as of questioning his indisputable right to lay down the law to all who agree with his great fundamental theorem—that the longest ear is the most competent to judge of metre. ***Habemus confitentem asinum.*]**

    Arrive that Sestos where my Hero lies.
    Countess. Nay, you'll do more; you'll make the river too
With their heartbloods that keep our love asunder;
Of which my husband and your wife are twain.
    Edward. Thy beauty makes them guilty of their death
And gives in evidence that they shall die;
Upon which verdict I their judge condemn them.
    Countess. O perjured beauty! more corrupted judge!
When, to the great star-chamber o'er our heads,
The universal sessions calls to count
This packing evil, we both shall tremble for it.
    Edward. What says my fair love? is she resolute?
    Countess. Resolute to be dissolved:[Note 1: A Latin pun, or rather a punning Latinism, not altogether out of Shakespeare's earliest line. But see the note preced-

ing this one] and, therefore, this;
> Keep but thy word, great king, and I am thine.
> Stand where thou dost; I'll part a little from thee;
> And see how I will yield me to thy hands.
> Here by my side do hang my wedding knives;
> Take thou the one, and with it kill thy queen,
> And learn by me to find her where she lies;
> And with the other I'll despatch my love,
> Which now lies fast asleep within my heart:
> When they are gone, then I'll consent to love.

Such genuinely good wine as this needs no bush. But from this point onwards I can find nothing especially commendable in the remainder of the scene except its brevity. The King of course abjures his purpose, and of course compares the Countess with Lucretia to the disadvantage of the Roman matron; summons his son, Warwick, and the attendant lords; appoints each man his post by sea or land; and starts for Flanders in a duly moral and military state of mind.

Here ends the first part of the play; and with it all possible indication, though never so shadowy, of the possible shadowy presence of Shakespeare. At the opening of the third act we are thrown among a wholly new set of characters and events, all utterly out of all harmony and keeping with all that has gone before. Edward alone survives as nominal protagonist; but this survival—as suredly not of the fittest—is merely the survival of the shadow of a name. Anything more pitifully crude and feeble, more helplessly inartistic and incomposite, than this process or pretence of juncture where there is no juncture, this infantine shifting and shuffling of the scenes and figures, it is impossible to find among the rudest and weakest attempts of the dawning or declining drama in its first or second childhood.

It is the less necessary to analyse at any length the three remaining acts of this play, that the work has already been done to my hand, and well done, by Charles Knight; who, though no professed critic or esoteric expert in Shakespearean letters, approved himself by dint of sheer honesty and conscience not unworthy of a considerate hearing. To his edition of Shakespeare I therefore refer all readers desirous of further excerpts than I care to give.

The first scene of the third act is a storehouse of contemporary commonplace. Nothing fresher than such stale pot-pourri as the following is to be gathered up in thin sprinklings from off the dry flat soil. A messenger informs the French king that he has descried off shore

> The proud armado (*sic*) of King Edward's ships;
> Which at the first, far off when I did ken,
> Seemed as it were a grove of withered pines;
> But, drawing on, their glorious bright aspect,
> Their streaming ensigns wrought of coloured silk,
> Like to a meadow full of sundry flowers,
> Adorns the naked bosom of the earth;

and so on after the exactest and therefore feeblest fashion of the Pre-Marlowites; with equal regard, as may be seen, for grammar and for sense in the construction of his periods. The narrative of a sea-fight ensuing on this is pitiable beyond pity and contemptibly beneath contempt.

In the next scene we have a flying view of peasants in flight, with a description of five cities on fire not undeserving of its place in the play, immediately after the preceding sea-piece: but relieved by such wealth of pleasantry as marks the following jest, in which the most purblind eye will be the quickest to discover a touch of the genuine Shakespearean humour.

> *1st Frenchman.* What, is it quarter-day, that you remove,
> And carry bag and baggage too?
> *2nd Frenchman.* Quarter-day? ay, and quartering-day, I fear.

Euge!

The scene of debate before Cressy is equally flat and futile, vulgar and verbose; yet in this Sham Shakespearean scene of our present poeticule's I have noted one genuine Shakespearean word, "solely singular for its singleness."

So may thy temples with Bellona's hand
Be still adorned with laurel victory!

In this notably inelegant expression of goodwill we find the same use of the word "laurel" as an adjective and epithet of victory which thus confronts us in the penultimate speech of the third scene in the first act of ***Antony and Cleopatra.***

Upon your sword
Sit laurel victory, and smooth success
Be strewed before your feet!

There is something more (as less there could not be) of spirit and movement in the battle-scene where Edward refuses to send relief to his son, wishing the prince to win his spurs unaided, and earn the firstfruits of his fame single-handed against the heaviest odds; but the forcible feebleness of a minor poet's fancy shows itself amusingly in the mock stoicism and braggart philosophy of the King's reassuring reflection, "We have more sons than one."

In the first and third scenes of the fourth act we may concede some slight merit to the picture of a chivalrous emulation in magnanimity between the Duke of Burgundy and his former fellow-student, whose refusal to break his parole as a prisoner extorts from his friend the concession refused to his importunity as an envoy: but the execution is by no means worthy of the subject.

The limp loquacity of long-winded rhetoric, so natural to men and soldiers in an hour of emergency, which distinguishes the dialogue between the Black Prince and Audley on the verge of battle, is relieved by this one last touch of quasi-Shakespearean thought or style discoverable in the play of which I must presently take a short—and a long—farewell.

Death's name is much more mighty than his deeds:
Thy parcelling this power hath made it more.
As many sands as these my hands can hold
Are but my handful of so many sands;
Then all the world—and call it but a power—
Easily ta'en up, and [Note 1: The simple substitution of the word "is" for the word "and" would rectify the grammar here—were that worth while.] quickly thrown away;
But if I stand to count them sand by sand.
The number would confound my memory
And make a thousand millions of a task
Which briefly is no more indeed than one.
These quartered squadrons and these regiments
Before, behind us, and on either hand,
Are but a power: When we name a man,
His hand, his foot, his head, have several strengths;
And being all but one self instant strength,
Why, all this many, Audley, is but one,
And we can call it all but one man's strength.
He that hath far to go tells it by miles;
If he should tell the steps, it kills his heart:
The drops are infinite that make a flood,
And yet, thou know'st, we call it but a rain.
There is but one France, one king of France, [Note 1: Qu. So there is but one France, etc.?]
That France hath no more kings; and that same king
Hath but the puissant legion of one king;
And we have one: Then apprehend no odds;
For one to one is fair equality.

Bien coupe, mal cousu; such is the most favourable verdict I can pass on this voluminous effusion of a spirit smacking rather of the schools than of the field. The first six lines or so might pass muster as the early handiwork of Shakespeare; the rest has as little of his manner as his matter, his metre as his style.

The poet can hardly be said to rise again after this calamitous collapse. We find in the rest of this scene nothing better worth remark than such poor catches at a word as this;

> And let those milkwhite messengers of time
> Show thy time's learning in this dangerous time;

a villainous trick of verbiage which went nigh now and then to affect the adolescent style of Shakespeare, and which happens to find itself as admirably as unconsciously burlesqued in two lines of this very scene:

> I will not give a penny for a life,
> Nor half a halfpenny to shun grim death.

The verses intervening are smooth, simple, and passably well worded; indeed the force of elegant commonplace cannot well go further than in such lines as these.

> Thyself art bruised and bent with many broils,
> And stratagems forepast with iron pens
> Are texed [Note 1: Non-Shakespearean.] in thine honourable face;
> Thou art a married man in this distress,
> But danger woos me as a blushing maid;
> Teach me an answer to this perilous time.
> *Audley.* To die is all as common as to live;
> The one in choice, the other holds in chase;
> For from the instant we begin to live
> We do pursue and hunt the time to die:
> First bud we, then we blow, and after seed;
> Then presently we fall; and as a shade

> Follows the body, so we follow death.
> If then we hunt for death, why do we fear it?
> If we fear it, why do we follow it?

(Let me intimate a doubt in passing, whether Shakespeare would ever have put by the mouth of any but a farcical mask a query so provocative of response from an Irish echo—"Because we can't help.")

> If we do fear, with fear we do but aid
> The thing we fear to seize on us the sooner;
> If we fear not, then no resolvèd proffer
> Can overthrow the limit of our fate:

and so forth. Again the hastiest reader will have been reminded of a passage in the transcendant central scenes of **Measure for Measure:**

> Merely, thou art death's fool;
> For him thou labour'st by thy flight to shun,
> And yet runn'st toward him still;

and hence also some may infer that this pitiful penny-whistle was blown by the same breath which in time gained power to fill that archangelic trumpet Credat Zoilus Shakespearomastix, non ego.

The next scene is something better than passable, but demands no special analysis and affords no necessary extract. We may just observe as examples of style the play on words between the flight of hovering ravens and the flight of routed soldiers, and the description of the sudden fog

> Which now hath hid the airy floor of heaven,
> And made at noon a night unnatural
> Upon the quaking and dismayèd world.

The interest rises again with the reappearance and release of Salisbury, and lifts the style for a moment to its own level. À tout seigneur tout honneur; the author deserves some dole of moderate approbation for his tribute to the national chivalry of a Frenchman as here exemplified in the person of Prince Charles.

Of the two next scenes, in which the battle of Poitiers is so inadequately "staged to the show," I can only say that if any reader believes them to be the possible work of the same hand which set before all men's eyes for all time the field of Agincourt, he will doubtless die in that belief, and go to his own place in the limbo of commentators.

But a yet more flagrant effect of contrast is thrust upon our notice at the opening of the fifth act. If in all the historical groundwork of this play there is one point of attraction which we might have thought certain to stimulate the utmost enterprise and evoke the utmost capacities of an aspiring dramatist, it must surely be sought in the crowning scene of the story; in the scene of Queen Philippa's intercession for the burgesses of Calais. We know how Shakespeare on the like occasion was wont to transmute into golden verse the silver speech supplied to him by North's version of Amyot's Plutarch.[Note 1: I choose for a parallel Shakespeare's use of Plutarch in the composition of his Roman plays rather than his use of Hall and Holinshed in the composition of his English histories, because Froissart is a model more properly to be set against Plutarch than against Holinshed or Hall] With the text of Lord Berners before him, the author of **King Edward III** has given us for the gold of Froissart not even adulterated copper, but unadulterated lead. Incredible as it may seem to readers of the historian, the poeticule has actually contrived so far to transfigure by dint of disfiguring him that this most noble and pathetic scene in all the annals of chivalry, when passed through the alembic of his incompetence, appears in a garb of transforming verse under a guise at once weak and wordy, coarse and unchivalrous. The whole scene is at all points alike in its unlikeness to the workmanship of Shakespeare.

Here then I think we may finally draw bridle: for the rest of the course is not worth running; there is nothing in the residue of this last act which deserves analysis or calls for commentary. We have now examined the whole main body of the work with somewhat more than necessary care; and our conclusion is simply this: that if any man of common reading, common modesty, common judgment, and common sense, can be found to maintain the theory of Shakespeare's possible partnership in the composition of this play, such a man will assuredly admit that the only discernible or imaginable touches of his hand are very slight, very few, and very early. For myself, I am and have always been perfectly satisfied with one single and simple piece of evidence that Shakespeare had not a finger in the concoction of *King Edward III* He was the author of *King Henry V.*

I WAS not surprised to hear that my essay on the historical play of *King Edward III.* had on its first appearance met in various quarters with assailants of various kinds. There are some forms of attack to which no answer is possible for a man of any human self-respect but the lifelong silence of contemptuous disgust To such as these I will never condescend to advert or to allude further than by the remark now as it were forced from me, that never once in my life have I had or will I have recourse in self-defence either to the blackguard's loaded bludgeon of personalities or to the dastard's sheathed dagger of disguise. I have reviled no man's person: I have outraged no man's privacy. When I have found myself misled either by imperfection of knowledge or of memory, or by too much confidence in a generally trustworthy guide, I have silently corrected the misquotation or readily repaired the error. To the successive and representative heroes of the undying Dunciad I have left and will always leave the foul use of their own foul weapons. I have spoken freely and fearlessly, and so shall on all occasions continue to speak, of what I find to be worthy of praise or dispraise, contempt or honour, in the public works and actions of men. Here ends and here has always ended in literary matters the proper province of a gentleman; beyond it, though sometimes intruded on in time past by trespassers of a nobler race, begins the proper province of a blackguard.

REPORT OF THE PROCEEDINGS ON THE FIRST ANNIVERSARY SESSION OF THE NEWEST SHAKESPEARE SOCIETY.

A PAPER was read by Mr. A. on the disputed authorship of *A Midsummer*

Night's Dream. He was decidedly of opinion that this play was to be ascribed to George Chapman. He based this opinion principally on the ground of style. From its similarity of subject he had at first been disposed to assign it to Cyril Tourneur, author of ***The Revenger's Tragedy;*** and he had drawn up in support of this theory a series of parallel passages extracted from the speeches of Vindice in that drama and of Oberon in the present play. He pointed out however that the character of Puck could hardly have been the work of any English poet but the author of ***Bussy d'Ambois.*** There was here likewise that gravity and condensation of thought conveyed through the medium of the "full and heightened style" commended by Webster, and that preponderance of philosophic or political discourse over poetic interest and dramatic action for which the author in question had been justly censured.

Some of the audience appearing slightly startled by this remark (indeed it afterwards appeared that the Chairman had been on the point of asking the learned member whether he was not thinking rather of *Love's Labour's Lost?*), Mr. A cited the well-known scene in which Oberon discourses with Puck on matters concerning Mary Stuart and Queen Elizabeth, instead of despatching him at once on his immediate errand. This was universally accepted as proof positive, and the reading concluded amid signs of unanimous assent, when

Mr. B. had nothing to urge against the argument they had just heard, but he must remind them that there was a more weighty kind of evidence than that adduced by Mr. A.; and to this he doubted not they would all defer. He could prove by a tabulated statement that the words "to" and "from" occurred on an average from seven to nine times in every play of Chapman; whereas in the play under consideration the word "to" occurred exactly twelve times and the word "from" precisely ten. He was therefore of opinion that the authorship should in all probability be assigned to Anthony Munday.

As nobody present could dispute this conclusion, Mr. C. proceeded to read the argument by which he proposed to establish the fact, hitherto unaccountably overlooked by all preceding commentators, that the character of Romeo was obviously designed as a satire on Lord Burghley. The first and perhaps the strongest evidence in favour of this proposition was the extreme difficulty, he might almost say the utter impossibility, of discovering a single point of likeness between the two characters. This would naturally be the first precaution taken by a poor player who designed to attack an all-powerful Minister. But more direct light was thrown upon the subject by a passage in which "that kind of fruit that maids call medlars when they laugh alone" is mentioned in connection with a wish of Romeo's regarding his mistress. This must evidently be taken to refer to some recent occasion on which the policy of Lord Burghley (possibly in the matter of the Anjou marriage) had been rebuked in private by the Maiden Queen, "his mistress," as meddling, laughable, and fruitless.

This discovery seemed to produce a great impression till the Chairman reminded the Society that the play in question was now generally ascribed to George Peele, who was notoriously the solicitor of Lord Burghley's patronage and the recipient of his bounty. That this poet was the author of **Romeo and Juliet** could no longer be a matter of doubt, as he was confident they would all agree with him on hearing that a living poet of note had positively assured him of the fact; adding that he had always thought so when at school. The plaudits excited by this announcement had scarcely subsided, when the Chairman clenched the matter by observing that he rather thought the same opinion had ultimately been entertained by his own grandmother.

Mr. D. then read a paper on the authorship and the hidden meaning of two contemporary plays which, he must regretfully remark, were too obviously calculated to cast a most unfavourable and even sinister light on the moral character of the new Shakespeare; whose possibly suspicious readiness to attack the vices of others with a view to diverting attention from his own was signally exemplified in the well-known fact that, even while putting on a feint of respect and tenderness for his memory, he had exposed the profligate haunts and habits of Christopher Marlowe under the transparent pseudonym of Christopher Sly. To the first of these plays attention had long since been drawn by a person of whom it was only necessary to say that he had devoted a long life to the study and illustration of Shakespeare and his age, and had actually presumed to publish a well-known edition of the poet at a date previous to the establishment of the present Society. He (Mr. D.) was confident that not another syllable could be necessary to expose that person to the contempt of all present. He proceeded, however, with the kind encouragement of the Chairman, to indulge at that editor's expense in sundry personalities both "loose and humorous," which being totally unfit for publication here are reserved for a private issue of "Loose and Humorous Papers" to be edited, with a running marginal commentary or illustrative and explanatory version of the utmost possible fullness, [Note 1: This word was incomprehensibly misprinted in the first issue of the Society's Report, where it appeared as "foulness." To prevent misapprehension, the whole staff of printers was at once discharged.] by the Founder and another member of the Society. To these it might possibly be undesirable for them to attract the notice of the outside world. Reverting therefore to his first subject from various references to the presumed private character, habits, gait, appearance, and bearing of the gentleman in question, Mr. D. observed that the ascription of a share in the *Taming of the Shrew* to William Haughton (hitherto supposed the author of a comedy called *Englishmen for my Money*) implied a doubly discreditable blunder. The real fact, as he would immediately prove, was not that Haughton was joint author with Shakespeare of the *Taming of the Shrew,* but that Shakespeare was joint author with Haughton of *Englishmen for my Money.* He would not enlarge on the obvious fact that Shakespeare, so notorious a plunderer of others, had actually been reduced to steal from his own poor store an image transplanted from the last scene of the third act of *Romeo and Juliet* into the last scene of the third act of *Englishmen for my Money;* where the well-known and pitiful phrase—"Night's candles are burnt out"—reappears in all its paltry vulgarity as follows; "Night's candles burn obscure." Ample as was the proof here supplied, he would prefer to rely exclusively upon such further evidence as might be said to lie at once on the surface and in a nutshell.

The second title of this play, by which the first title was in a few years totally superseded, ran thus: *A Woman will have her Will.* Now even in an age of punning titles such as that of a well-known and delightful treatise by Sir John Harrington, the peculiar fondness of Shakespeare for puns was notorious; but especially for puns on names, as in the proverbial case of Sir Thomas Lucy; and above all for puns on his own Christian name, as in his 135th, 136th, and 143rd sonnets. It must now be but too evident to the meanest intelligence—to the meanest intelligence, he repeated; for to such only did he or would he then and there or ever or anywhere address himself—(loud applause) that the graceless author, more utterly lost to all sense of shame than any Don Juan or other typical libertine of fiction, had come forward to placard by way of self-advertisement on his own stage, and before the very eyes of a Maiden Queen, the scandalous confidence in his own powers of fascination and seduction so cynically expressed in the too easily intelligible vaunt—A Woman will have her Will [Shakespeare]. In the penultimate line of the hundred and forty-third sonnet the very phrase might be said to occur:—

So will I pray that thou mayst have thy Will.

Having thus established his case in the first instance to the satisfaction, as he trusted, not only of the present Society, but of any asylum for incurables in any part of the country, the learned member now passed on to the consideration of the allusions at once to Shakespeare and to a celebrated fellow-countryman, fellow-poet, and personal friend of his—Michael Drayton—contained in a play which had been doubtfully attributed to Shakespeare himself by such absurd idiots as looked rather to the poetical and dramatic quality of a poem or a play than to such tests as those to which alone any member of that Society would ever dream of appealing. What these were he need not specify; it was enough to say in recommendation of them that they had rather less to do with any question of dramatic or other poetry than with the differential calculus or the squaring of the circle. It followed that only the most perversely ignorant and æsthetically presumptuous of readers could imagine the possibility of Shakespeare's concern or partnership in a play which had Ho more Shakespearean quality about it than mere poetry, mere passion, mere pathos, mere beauty and vigour of thought and language, mere command of dramatic effect, mere depth and sobriety of power to read, interpret, and reproduce the secrets of the heart and spirit Could any further evidence be required of the unfitness and unworthiness to hold or to utter any opinion on the matter in hand which had consistently been displayed by die poor creatures to whom he had just referred, it would be found, as he felt sure the Founder and all worthy members of their Society would be the first to admit, in the despicable diffidence, the pitiful modesty, the contemptible deficiency in common assurance, with which the suggestion of Shakespeare's partnership in this play had generally been put forward and backed up. The tragedy of *Arden of Feversham* was indeed connected with Shakespeare—and that, as he should proceed to show, only too intimately; but Shakespeare was not connected with it—that is, in the capacity of its author. In what capacity would be but too evident when he mentioned the names of the two leading ruffians concerned in the murder of the principal character—Black Will and Shakebag. The single original of these two characters he need scarcely pause to point out. It would be observed that a double precaution had been taken against any charge of libel or personal attack which might be brought against the author and supported by the all-powerful court influence of Shakespeare's two principal patrons, the Earls of Essex and Southampton. Two figures were substituted for one, and the unmistakable name of Will Shakebag was cut in half and divided between them. Care had moreover been taken to disguise the person by altering the complexion of the individual aimed at. That the actual Shakespeare was a fair man they had the evidence of the coloured bust at Stratford. Could any capable and fair-minded man—he would appeal to their justly honoured Founder—require further evidence as to the original of Black Will Shakebag? Another important character in the play was Black Will's accomplice and Arden's servant—Michael, after whom the play had also at one time been called *Murderous Michael.* The single fact that Shakespeare and Drayton were both of them Warwickshire men would suffice, he could not doubt, to carry conviction with it to the mind of every member present, with regard to the original of this personage. It now only remained for him to produce the name of the real author of this play. He would do so at once—Ben Jonson. About the time of its production Jonson was notoriously engaged in writing those additions to the ***Spanish Tragedy*** of which a preposterous attempt had been made to deprive him on the paltry ground that the style (forsooth) of these additional scenes was very like the style of Shakespeare and utterly unlike the style of Jonson. To dispose for ever of this pitiful argument it would be sufficient to mention the names of its two first and principal supporters—Charles Lamb and Samuel Taylor Coleridge (hisses and laughter). Now, in these "adycions to Jeronymo" a painter was introduced complaining of the murder of his son. In the play before them a painter was introduced as an accomplice in the murder of Arden. It was unnecessary to dwell upon so trivial a point of difference as that between the stage employment or the moral character of the one artist and the other. In either case they were as closely as possible connected with a murder. There was a painter in the ***Spanish Tragedy,***, and there was also a painter in ***Arden of Feversham.*** He need not—he would not add another word in confirmation of the now established fact, that Ben Jonson had in this play held up to perpetual infamy—whether deserved or undeserved he would not pretend to say—the names of two poets who afterwards became his friends, but whom he had previously gibbeted or at least pilloried in public as Black Will Shakespeare and Murderous Michael Drayton.

Mr. E. then brought forward a subject of singular interest and importance—"The lameness of Shakespeare—was it moral or physical?" He would not insult their intelligence by dwelling on the absurd and exploded hypothesis that this expression was allegorical, but would at once assume that the infirmity in question was physical. Then arose the question—In which leg? He was prepared, on the evidence of an early play, to prove to demonstration that the injured and interesting limb was the left "This shoe is my father," says Launce in the ***Two Gentlemen of Verona;*** "no, this left shoe is my father; no, no, this left shoe is my mother; nay, that cannot be so neither; yes, it is so, it is so; ***it hath the worser sole"*** This passage was not necessary either to the progress of the play or to the development of the character; he believed he was justified in asserting that it was not borrowed from the original novel on which the play was founded; the inference was obvious, that without some personal allusion it must have been as unintelligible to the audience as it had hitherto been to the commentators. His conjecture was confirmed, and the whole subject illustrated with a new light, by the well-known line in one of the Sonnets, in which the poet describes himself as "made lame by Fortune's dearest spite": a line of which the inner meaning and personal application had also by a remarkable chance been reserved for him (Mr. E.)to discover. There could be no doubt that we had here a clue to the origin of the physical infirmity referred to; an accident which must have befallen Shakespeare in early life while acting at the Fortune theatre, and consequently before his connection with a rival company; a fact of grave importance till now unverified. The epithet "dearest," like so much else in the Sonnets, was evidently susceptible of a double interpretation. The first and most natural explanation of the term would at once suggest itself; the playhouse would of necessity be dearest to the actor dependent on it for subsistence, as the means of getting his bread; but he thought it not unreasonable to infer from this unmistakable allusion that the entrance fee charged at the Fortune may probably have been higher than the price of seats in any other house. Whether or not this fact, taken in conjunction with the accident already mentioned, should be assumed as the immediate cause of Shakespeare's subsequent change of service, he was not prepared to pronounce with such positive confidence as they might naturally expect from a member of the Society; but he would take upon himself to affirm that his main thesis was now and for ever established on the most irrefragable evidence, and that no assailant could by any possibility dislodge by so much as a hair's breadth the least fragment of a single brick in the impregnable structure of proof raised by the argument to which they had just listened.

This demonstration being thus satisfactorily concluded, Mr. F. proceeded to read his paper on the date of *Othello,* and on the various parts of that play respectively assignable to Samuel Rowley, to George Wilkins, and to Robert Daborne. It was evident that the story of Othello and Desdemona was originally quite distinct from that part of the play in which Iago was a leading figure. This he was prepared to show at some length by means of the weak-ending test, the light-ending test, the double-ending test, the triple-ending test, the heavy-monosyllabic-eleventh-syllable-of-the-double-ending test, the run-on-line test, and the central-pause test. Of the partnership of other poets in the play he was able to adduce a simpler but not less cogent proof. A member of their Committee said to an objector lately: "To me, there are the handwritings of four different men, the thoughts and powers of four different men, in the play. If you can't see them now, you must wait till, by study, you can. I can't give you eyes." To this argument he (Mr. F.) felt that it would be an insult to their understandings if he should attempt to add another word. Still, for those who were willing to try and learn, and educate their ears and eyes, he had prepared six tabulated statements—

(At this important point of a most interesting paper, our reporter unhappily became unconscious, and remained for some considerable period in a state of death-like stupor. On recovering from this total and unaccountable suspension of all his faculties, he found the speaker drawing gradually near the end of his figures, and so far succeeded in shaking off the sense of coma as to be able to resume his notes.)

That the first and fourth scenes of the third act were not by the same hand as the third scene he should have no difficulty in proving to the satisfaction of all capable and fair-minded men. In the first and fourth scenes the word "virtuous" was used as a dissyllable; in the third it was used as a trisyllable.

"Is, that she will to virtuous Desdemona." iii. 1.

"Where virtue is, these are more virtuous." iii. 3.

"That by your virtuous means I may again." iii. 4.

In the third scene he would also point out the great number of triple endings which had originally led the able editor of Euclid's Elements of Geometry to attribute the authorship of this scene to Shirley: **Cassio** (twice), **patience, Cassio** (again), **discretion, Cassio** (again), **honesty, Cassio** (again), **jealousy, jealous** (used as a trisyllable in the verse of Shakespeare's time), **company** (two consecutive lines with the triple ending), **Cassio** (again), **conscience, petition, ability, importunity, conversation, marriage, dungeon, mandragora, passion, monstrous, conclusion, bounteous.** He could not imagine any man in his senses questioning the weight of this evidence. Now, let them take the rhymed speeches of the Duke and Brabantio in Act i. Sc 3, and compare them with the speech of Othello in Act iv. Sc 2,

> Had it pleased heaven
> To try me with affliction.

He appealed to any expert whether this was not in Shakespeare's easy fourth budding manner, with, too, various other points already touched on. On the other hand, take the opening of Brabantio's speech—

So let the Turk of Cyprus us beguile;
We lose it not so long as we can smile.

That, he said, was in Shakespeare's difficult second flowering manner—the style of the later part of the earlier stage of Shakespeare's rhetorical first period but one. It was no more possible to move the one passage up to the date of the other than to invert the order of the alphabet. Here, then, putting aside for the moment the part of the play supplied by Shakespeare's assistants in the last three acts—miserably weak some of it was—they were able to disentangle the early love-play from the later work in which Iago was principally concerned. There was at least fifteen years' growth between them, the steps of which could be traced in the poet's intermediate plays by any one who chose to work carefully enough at them. Set any of the speeches addressed in the Shakespeare part of the last act by Othello to Desdemona beside the consolatory address of the Duke to Brabantio, and see the difference of the rhetoric and style in the two. If they turned to characters, Othello and Desdemona were even more clearly the companion pair to Biron and Rosaline of *Love's Labours Lost* than were Falstaff and Doll Tearsheet the match-pair (*sic*) of Romeo and Juliet. In *Love's Labour's Lost* the question of complexion was identical, though the parts were reversed. He would cite but a few parallel passages in evidence of this relationship between the subjects of the two plays.

Love's Labour's Lost, iv. 3.

1. "By heaven, thy love is black as ebony."
2. "No face *is fair* that is not full so black."
3. "O paradox! Black is the badge of hell."
4. "O, *if* in black my lady's brows be decked."
5. "And therefore is she born to make black fair."
6. "Paints itself black to imitate her brow."
7. "To look like her are **chimney-sweepers** black."

Othello.

1. "An old black ram." i. 1.
2. "Your son-in-law is far more *fair* than black." i. 3.
3. "How if she be black and witty?" ii. 1.
4. "*If* she be black, and thereto have a wit." id.
5. "A measure to the health of black Othello." ii. 3.
6. "For I am black." ii 3.
7. "*Begrimed* and black." id.

Now, with these parallel passages before them, what man, woman, or child could bring himself or herself to believe that the connection of these plays was casual or the date of the first **Othello** removable from the date of the early contemporary late-first-period-but-one play **Love's Labours Lost,** or that anybody's opinion that they were so was worth one straw? When therefore by the introduction of the Iago episode Shakespeare in his later days had with the assistance of three fellow-poets completed the unfinished work of his youth, the junction thus effected of the Brabantio part of the play with this Iago underplot supplied them with an evidence wholly distinct from that of the metrical test which yet confirmed in every point the conclusion independently arrived at and supported by the irresistible coincidence of all the tests. He defied anybody to accept his principle of study or adopt his method of work, and arrive at a different conclusion from himself.

The reading of Mr. G.'s paper on the authorship of the soliloquies in **Hamlet** was unavoidably postponed till the next meeting, the learned member having only time on this occasion to give a brief summary of the points he was prepared to establish and the grounds on which he was prepared to establish them. A year or two since, when he first thought of starting the present Society, he had never read a line of the play in question, having always understood it to be admittedly spurious: but on being assured of the contrary by one of the two foremost poets of the English-speaking world, who was good enough to read out to him in proof of this assertion all that part of the play which could reasonably be assigned to Shakespeare, he had of course at once surrendered his own former opinion, well grounded as it had hitherto seemed to be on the most solid of all possible foundations. At their next meeting he would show cause for attributing to Ben Jonson not only the soliloquies usually but inconsiderately quoted as Shakespeare's, but the entire original conception of the character of the Prince of Denmark. The resemblance of this character to that of Volpone in *The Fox* and to that of Face in *The Alchemist* could not possibly escape the notice of the most cursory reader. The principle of disguise was the same in each case, whether the end in view were simply personal profit, or (as in the case of Hamlet) personal profit combined with revenge; and whether the disguise assumed was that of madness, of sickness, or of a foreign personality, the assumption of character was in all three cases identical. As to style, he was only too anxious to meet (and, he doubted not, to beat) on his own ground any antagonist whose ear had begotten [Note 1: When the learned member made use of this remarkable phase he probably had in his mind the suggestive query of Agnès, *si les enfants qu'on fait se faisaient par l'oreille?* But the flower of rhetoric here gathered was beyond the reach of Arnolphe's innocent ward. The procreation in such a case is even more difficult for fancy to realise than the conception.] the crude and untenable theory that the Hamlet soliloquies were not distinctly within the range of the man who could produce those of Crites and of Macilente in *Cynthia's Revels* and *Every Man out of his Humour.* The author of those soliloquies could, and did, in the parallel passages of *Hamlet,* rise near the height of the master he honoured and loved.

The further discussion of this subject was reserved for the next meeting of the Society, as was also the reading of Mr. H.'s paper on the subsequent quarrel between the two joint authors of *Hamlet,* which led to Jonson's caricature of Shakespeare (then retired from London society to a country life of solitude) under the name of Morose, and to Shakespeare's retort on Jonson, who was no less evidently attacked under the designation of Ariel. The allusions to the subject of Shakespeare's sonnets in the courtship and marriage of Epicœne by Morose were as obvious as the allusions in the part of Ariel to the repeated incarceration of Jonson, first on a criminal and secondly on a political charge, and to his probable release in the former case (during the reign of Elizabeth=Sycorax) at the intercession of Shakespeare, who was allowed on all hands to have represented himself in the character of Prospero ("it was mine art that let thee out"). Mr. I. would afterwards read a paper on the evidence for Shakespeare's whole or part authorship of a dozen or so of the least known plays of his time, which, besides having various words and phrases in common with his acknowledged works, were obviously too bad to be attributed to any other known writer of the period. Eminent among these was the tragedy of ***Andromana, or the Merchant's Wife,*** long since rejected from the list of Shirley's works as unworthy of that poet's hand. Unquestionably it was so; not less unworthy than ***A Larum for London*** of Marlowe's. The consequent inference that it must needs be the work of the new Shakespeare's was surely no less cogent in this than in the former case. The allusion occurring in it to a play bearing date just twenty-six years after the death of Shakespeare, and written by a poet then unborn, was a strong point in favour of his theory. (This argument was received with general marks of adhesion.) What, he would ask, could be more natural than that Shirley when engaged on the revision and arrangement for the stage of this posthumous work of the new Shakespeare's (a fact which could require no further proof than he had already adduced), should have inserted this reference in order to disguise the name of its real author, and protect it from the disfavour of an audience with whom that name was notoriously out of fashion? This reasoning, conclusive in itself, became even more irresistible—or would become so, if that were anything less than an absolute impossibility—on comparison of parallel passages.

> Though kings still hug suspicion in their bosoms,
> They hate the causer. (***Andromana,*** Act i. Sc. 3.)

Compare this with the avowal put by Shakespeare into the mouth of a king.

> Though I did wish him dead
> I hate the murderer. (***King Richard II.,*** Act v. Sc. 6.)

Again in the same scene:

> For then her husband comes home from the Rialto.

Compare this with various passages (too familiar to quote) in the ***Merchant of Venice.*** The transference of the Rialto to Iberia was of a piece with the discovery of a sea-coast in Bohemia. In the same scene Andromana says to her lover, finding him reluctant to take his leave, almost in the very words of Romeo to Juliet,

> Then let us stand and outface danger,
> Since you will have it so.

It was obvious that only the author of the one passage could have thought it necessary to disguise his plagiarism in the other by an inversion of sexes between the two speakers. In the same scene were three other indisputable instances of repetition.

> Mariners might with far greater ease
> Hear whole shoals of sirens singing.

Compare *Comedy of Errors,* Act iii. Scene 2.

> Sing, siren, for thyself.

In this case identity of sex was as palpable an evidence for identity of authorship as diversity of sex had afforded in the preceding instance.

Again:

> Have oaths no *more validity* with princes?

In *Romeo and Juliet,* Act iii. Scene 3, the very same words were coupled in the very same order:

> *More validity,*

> More honourable state, more courtship lies
> In carrion flies than Romeo.

Again:

It would have killed a salamander.

Compare the *First Part of King Henry IV.,* Act iii. Scene 3.

I have maintained that salamander of yours with fire any time this two and thirty years.

In Act ii. Scene 2 the hero, on being informed how heavy are the odds against him in the field, answers,

I am glad on't; the honour is the greater.

To which his confidant rejoins:
The danger is the greater.

And in the sixth scene of the same act the messenger observes:

I only heard the prince wish
He had fewer by a thousand men.

Could any member doubt that we had here the same hand which gave us the like debate between King Henry and Westmoreland on the eve of Agincourt? or could any member suppose that in the subsequent remark of the same military confidant, "I smell a rat, sir," there was merely a fortuitous coincidence with Hamlet's reflection as he "whips out his rapier"—in itself a martial proceeding—under similar circumstances to the same effect?

In the very next scene a captain observes of his own troops

Methinks such tattered rogues should never conquer:

a touch that could only be due to the pencil which had drawn Falstaff's ragged regiment. In both cases, moreover, it was to be noted that the tattered rogues proved ultimately victorious. But he had—they might hardly: believe it, but so it was—even yet stronger and more convincing evidence to offer. It would be remembered that a play called *The Double Falsehood,* formerly attributed to Shakespeare on the authority of Theobald, was now generally supposed to have been in its original form the work of Shirley. What, then, he would ask, could be more natural or more probable than that a play formerly ascribed to Shirley should prove to be the genuine work of Shakespeare? Common sense, common reason, common logic, all alike and all equally combined to enforce upon every candid judgment this inevitable conclusion. This, however, was nothing in comparison to the final: proof which he had yet to lay before them. He need not remind them that in the opinion of their illustrious German teachers, the first men to discover and reveal to his unworthy countrymen the very existence of the new Shakespeare, the authenticity of any play ascribed to the possibly too prolific pen of that poet was invariably to be determined in the last resort by consideration of its demerits. No English critic, therefore, who felt himself worthy to have been born a German, would venture to question the postulate on which all sound principles of criticism with regard to this subject must infallibly be founded: that, given any play of unknown or doubtful authorship, the worse it was, the likelier was it to be Shakespeare's. (This proposition was received with every sign of unanimous assent.) Now, on this ground he was prepared to maintain that the claims of *Andromana* to their most respectful, their most cordial, their most unhesitating acceptance were absolutely beyond all possibility of parallel. Not *Mucedorus* or *Fair Em,* not *The Birth of Merlin* or *Thomas Lord Cromwell,* could reasonably or fairly be regarded as on the same level of worthlessness with this incomparable production. No mortal man who had survived its perusal could for a moment hesitate to agree that it was the most incredibly, ineffably, inconceivably, unmitigatedly, irredeemably, inexpressibly damnable piece of bad work ever perpetrated by human hand. No mortal critic of the genuine Anglo-German school could therefore hesitate for a moment to agree that in common consistency he was bound to accept it as the possible work of no human hand but the hand of the New Shakespeare.

The Chairman then proceeded to recapitulate the work done and the benefits conferred by the Society during the twelve months which had elapsed since its foundation on that day (April 1st) last year. They had sample reason to congratulate themselves and him on the result. They had established an entirely new kind of criticism, working by entirely new means towards an entirely new end, in honour of an entirely new kind of Shakespeare. They had proved to demonstration and overwhelmed with obloquy the incompetence, the imbecility, the untrustworthiness, the blunders, the forgeries, the inaccuracies, the obliquities, the utter moral and literary worthlessness, of previous students and societies. They had revealed to the world at large the generally prevalent ignorance of Shakespeare and his works which so discreditably distinguished his countrymen. This they had been enabled to do by the simple process of putting forward various theories, and still more various facts, but all of equally incontrovertible value and relevance, of which no Englishman—he might say, no mortal—outside the Society had ever heard or dreamed till now. They had discovered the one trustworthy and indisputable method, so easy and so simple that it must now seem wonderful it should never have been discovered before, by which to pluck out the heart of the poet's mystery and detect the secret of his touch; the study of Shakespeare by rule of thumb. Every man, woman, and child born with five fingers on each hand was henceforward better qualified as a critic than any poet or scholar of time past. But it was not, whatever outsiders might pretend to think, exclusively on the verse-test, as it had facetiously been called on account of its total incompatibility with any conceivable scheme of metre or principle of rhythm—it was not exclusively on this precious and unanswerable test that they relied. Within the Society as well as without, the pretensions of those who would acknowledge no other means of deciding on debated questions had been refuted and repelled. What were the other means of investigation and verification in which not less than in the metrical test they were accustomed to put their faith; and by which they doubted not to, attain in the future even more remarkable results than their researches had as yet achieved, the debate just concluded, in common with every other for which they ever had met or ever were likely to meet, would amply suffice to show. By such processes as had been applied on this as on all occasions to the text of Shakespeare's works and the traditions of his life, they trusted in a very few years to subvert all theories which had hitherto been held and extirpate all ideas which had hitherto been cherished on the subject: and having thus cleared the ground for his advent, to discover for the admiration of the world, as the name of their Society implied, a New Shakespeare. The first step towards this end must of course be the demolition of the old one; and he would venture to say they had already made a good beginning in that direction. They had disproved or they would disprove the claim of Shakespeare to the sole authorship of Macbeth, Julius Cœsar, King Lear, Hamlet, *and* Othello; *they had established or they would establish the fact of his partnership in* Locrine, Mucedorus, The Birth of Merlin, Dr. Dodipoll, *and* Sir Giles Goosecap. *They had with them the incomparable critics of Germany; men whose knowledge and judgment on all questions of English literature were as far beyond the reach of their English followers as the freedom and enlightenment enjoyed by the subjects of a military empire were beyond the reach of the citizens of a democratic republic. They had established and affiliated to their own primitive body or church various branch societies or sects, in England and elsewhere, devoted to the pursuit of the same end by the same means and method of study as had just been exemplified in the transactions of the present meeting. Still there remained much to be done; in witness of which he proposed to lay before them at their next meeting, by way of inauguration under a happy omen of their new year's work, the complete body of evidence by means of which he was prepared to demonstrate that some considerable portion, if not the greater part, of the remaining plays hitherto assigned to Shakespeare was due to the collaboration of a contemporary actor and playwright, well known by name, but hitherto insufficiently appreciated; Robert Armin, the author of* A Nest of Ninnies.

ADDITIONS AND CORRECTIONS.

THE humble but hard-working journeyman of letters who was charged with the honourable duty of reporting the transactions at the last meeting of the Newest Shakespeare Society on the auspicious occasion of its first anniversary, April 1st, has received sundry more or less voluminous communications from various gentlemen whose papers were then read or announced, pointing out with more or less acrimonious commentary the matters on which it seems to them severally that they have cause to complain of imperfection or inaccuracy in his conscientious and painstaking report. Anxious above all things to secure for himself such credit as may be due to the modest merit of scrupulous fidelity, he desires to lay before the public so much of the corrections conveyed in their respective letters of reclamation as may be necessary to complete or to rectify the first draught of their propositions as conveyed in his former summary. On the present occasion, however, he must confine himself to forwarding the rectifications supplied by two of the members who took a leading part in the debate of April 1st.

The necessarily condensed report of Mr. A.'s paper on *A Midsummer Nights Dream* may make the reasoning put forward by that gentleman liable to the misconception of a hasty reader. The omission of various qualifying phrases has left his argument without such explanation, his statements without such reservation, as he had been careful to supply. He did not say in so many words that he had been disposed to assign this drama to the author of *The Revenger's Tragedy* simply on the score of the affinity discernible between the subjects of the two plays. He is not prone to self-confidence or to indulgence in paradox. What he did say was undeniable by any but those who trusted only to their ear, and refused to correct the conclusions thus arrived at by the help of other organs which God had given them—their fingers, for example, and their toes; by means of which a critic of trained and competent scholarship might with the utmost confidence count up as far as twenty, to the great profit of all students who were willing to accept his guidance and be bound by his decision on matters of art and poetry. Only the most purblind could fail to observe, what only the most perverse could hesitate to admit, that there was at first sight an obvious connection between the poison-flower—"purple from love's wound"—squeezed by Oberon into the eyes of the sleeping Titania and the poison rubbed by Vindice upon the skull of the murdered Gloriana. No student of Ulrici's invaluable work would think this a farfetched reference. That eminent critic had verified the meaning and detected the allusion underlying many a passage of Shakespeare in which the connection of moral idea was more difficult to establish than this. In the fifth act of either play there was a masque or dramatic show of a sanguinary kind; in the one case the bloodshed was turned to merry-making, in the other the merry-making was turned to bloodshed. Oberon's phrase, "till I torment thee for this injury," might easily be mistaken for a quotation from the part of Vindice. This explanation, he trusted, would suffice to exonerate his original view from any charge of haste or rashness; especially as he had now completely given it up, and adopted one (if possible) more impregnably based on internal and external evidence.

Mr. C. was not unnaturally surprised and indignant to find his position as to Romeo and Lord Burghley barely indicated, and the notice given of the arguments by which it was supported so docked and curtailed as to convey a most inadequate conception of their force. Among the chief points of his argument were these: that the forsaken Rosaline was evidently intended for the late Queen Mary, during whose reign Cecil had notoriously conformed to the observances of her creed, though ready on the accession of Elizabeth to throw it overboard at a day's notice; (it was not to be overlooked that the friar on first hearing the announcement of this change of faith is made earnestly to remonstrate, prefacing his reproaches with an invocation of two sacred names—an invocation peculiar to Catholics;) that the resemblance between old Capulet and Henry VIII, is obvious to the most careless reader; his oath of "God's bread!" immediately followed by the avowal "it makes me mad" is an unmistakable allusion to the passions excited by the eucharistic controversy; his violence towards Juliet at the end of the third act at once suggests the alienation of her father's heart from the daughter of Anne Boleyn; the self-congratulation on her own "stainless" condition as a virgin expressed by Juliet in soliloquy (Act iii. Sc. 2) while in the act of awaiting her bridegroom conveys a furtive stroke of satire at the similar vaunt of Elizabeth when likewise meditating marriage and preparing to receive a suitor from the hostile house of Valois. It must be unnecessary to point out the resemblance or rather the identity between the character and fortune of Paris and the character and fortune of Essex, whose fate had been foreseen and whose end prefigured by the poet with almost prophetic sagacity. To the far-reaching eye of Shakespeare it must have seemed natural and inevitable. that Paris (Essex) should fall by the hand of Romeo (Burghley) immediately before the monument of the Capulets where their common mistress was interred alive—immediately, that is, before the termination of the Tudor dynasty in the person of

Elizabeth, who towards the close of her reign may fitly have been regarded as one already buried with her fathers, though yet living in a state of suspended animation under the influence of a deadly narcotic potion administered by the friends of Romeo—by the partisans, that is, of the Cecilian policy. The Nurse was not less evidently designed to represent the Established Church. Allusions to the marriage of the clergy are profusely scattered through her speeches. Her deceased husband was probably meant for Sir Thomas More—"a merry man" to the last moment of his existence—who might well be supposed by a slight poetic license to have foreseen in the infancy of Elizabeth her future backsliding and fall from the straight path "when she came to age." The passing expression of tenderness with which the Nurse refers to his memory—"God be with his soul!"—implies at once the respect in which the name of the martyr Chancellor was still generally held, and the lingering remains of Catholic tradition which still made a prayer for the dead rise naturally to Anglican lips. On the other hand, the strife between Anglicans and Puritans, the struggle of episcopalian with Calvinistic reformers, was quite as plainly typified in the quarrel between the Nurse and Mercutio, in which the Martin Marprelate controversy was first unmistakably represented on the stage. The "saucy merchant, that was so full of his ropery," with his ridicule of the "stale" practice of Lenten fasting and abstinence, his contempt for "a Lenten pie," and his preference for a flesh diet as "very good meat in Lent," is clearly a disciple of Calvin; and the impotence of the Nurse, however scandalised at the nakedness of his ribald profanity, to protect herself against it by appeal to reason or tradition, is dwelt upon with an emphasis sufficient to indicate the secret tendency of the poet's own sympathies and convictions. In Romeo's attempt at conciliation, and his poor excuse for Mercutio (which yet the Nurse, an emblem of the temporising and accommodating pliancy of episcopalian Protestantism, shows herself only too ready to accept as valid) as "one that God hath made, for himself to mar,"—the allusion here is evidently to the democratic and revolutionary tendencies of the doctrine of Knox and Calvin, with its ultimate developments of individualism and private judgment—we recognise the note of Burghley's lifelong policy and its endeavour to fuse the Protestant or Puritan party with the state Church of the Tudors as by law established. The distaste of Elizabeth's bishops for such advances, their flutter of apprehension at the daring and their burst of indignation at the insolence of the Calvinists, are significantly expressed in terms which seem to hint at a possible return for help and protection to the shelter of the older faith and the support of its partisans. "An 'a speak anything against me, I'll take him down an 'a were lustier than he is, and twenty such Jacks;" (the allusion here is again obvious, to the baptismal name of John Calvin and John Knox, if not also to the popular byword of Jack Presbyter;) "and if I cannot," (here the sense of insecurity and dependence on foreign help or secular power becomes transparent) "I'll find those that shall." She disclaims communion with the Protestant Churches of the continent, with Amsterdam or Geneva: "I am none of his flirt-gills; I am none of his skains-mates." Peter, who carries her fan ("to hide her face: for her fan's the fairer face"; we may take this to be a symbol of the form of episcopal consecration still retained in the Anglican Church as a cover for its separation from Catholicism), is undoubtedly meant for Whitgift, Archbishop of Canterbury; the name Peter, as applied to a menial who will stand by and suffer every knave to use the Church at his pleasure, but is ready to draw as soon as another man if only he may be sure of having the secular arm of the law on his side, implies a bitter sarcasm on the intruding official of state then established by law as occupant of a see divorced from its connection with that of the apostle. The sense of instability natural to an institution which is compelled to rely for support on ministers who are themselves dependent on the state whose pay they draw for power to strike a blow in self-defence could hardly be better expressed than by the solemn and piteous, almost agonised asseveration; "Now, afore God, I am so vexed, that every part about me quivers." To Shakespeare, it cannot be doubted, the impending dissolution or dislocation of the Anglican system in "every part" by civil war and religious discord must even then have been but too ominously evident.

If further confirmation could be needed of the underlying significance of allusion traceable throughout this play, it might amply be supplied by fresh reference to the first scene in which the Nurse makes her appearance on the stage, and is checked by Lady Capulet in the full tide of affectionate regret for her lost husband. We can well imagine Anne Boleyn cutting short the regrets of some indiscreet courtier for Sir Thomas More in the very words of the text;

Enough of this; I pray thee, hold thy peace.

The "parlous knock" which left so big a lump upon the brow of the infant Juliet is evidently an allusion to the declaration of Elizabeth's illegitimacy while yet in her cradle. The seal of bastardy set upon the baby brow of Anne Boleyn's daughter may well be said to have "broken" it.

The counsel of the Nurse to Juliet in Act iii. Scene 5 to forsake Romeo for Paris indicates the bias of the hierarchy in favour of Essex—"a lovely gentleman"—rather than of the ultra-Protestant policy of Burghley, who doubtless in the eyes of courtiers and churchmen was "a dish-clout to him."

These were a few of the points, set down at random, which he had been enabled to verify within the limits of a single play. They would suffice to give an idea of the process by which, when applied in detail to every one of Shakespeare's plays, he trusted to establish the secret history and import of each, not less than the general sequence and significance of all. Further instalments of this work would probably be issued in the forthcoming or future Transactions of the Newest Shakespeare Society; and it was confidently expected that the final monument of his research, when thoroughly completed and illustrated by copious appendices, would prove as worthy as any work of mere English scholarship could hope to be of a place beside the inestimable commentaries of Gervinus, Ulrici, and the Polypseudocriticopantodapomorosophisti-cometricoglossematographicomaniacal Company for the Confusion of Shakespeare and Diffusion of Verbiage (Unlimited).

CHIMÆRA BOMBINANS IN VACUO.

NOTE.

MINDFUL of the good old apologue regarding "the squeak of the real pig," I think it here worth while to certify the reader of little faith, that the more incredibly impudent absurdities above cited are not so much or so often the freaks of parody or the fancies of burlesque as select excerpts and transcripts of printed and published utterances from the "pink soft litter" of a living brood—from the reports of an actual Society, issued in an abridged and doubtless an emasculated form through the columns of a weekly newspaper. One final and unapproachable instance, one transcendant and pyramidal example of classical taste and of critical scholarship, I did not venture to impair by transference from those columns and transplantation into these pages among humbler specimens of minor monstrosity. Let it stand here once more on record as "a good jest for ever"—or rather as the best and therefore as the worst, as the worst and therefore as the best, of all possible bad jests ever to be cracked between this and the crack of doom. Sophocles, said a learned member, was the proper parallel to Shakespeare among the ancient tragedians: Æschylus—hear, O heaven, and give ear, O earth!—Æschylus was only a Marlowe.

The hand which here transcribes this most transcendant utterance has written before now many lines in verse end in prose to the honour and glory of Christopher Marlowe: it has never—be the humble avowal thus blushingly recorded—it has never set down as the writer's opinion that he was only an Æschylus. In other words, it has never registered as my deliberate and judicial verdict the finding that he was only the equal of the greatest among all tragic and all prophetic poets; of the man who combined all the light of the Greeks with all the fire of the Hebrews; who varied at his will the revelation of the single gift of Isaiah with the display of the mightiest among the manifold gifts of Shakespeare.

THE END.

www.bookjungle.com *email: sales@bookjungle.com fax: 630-214-0564 mail: Book Jungle PO Box 2226 Champaign, IL 61825*

The Codes Of Hammurabi And Moses
W. W. Davies

QTY

The discovery of the Hammurabi Code is one of the greatest achievements of archaeology, and is of paramount interest, not only to the student of the Bible, but also to all those interested in ancient history...

Religion **ISBN:** *1-59462-338-4* **Pages:132**
MSRP $12.95

The Theory of Moral Sentiments
Adam Smith

QTY

This work from 1749. contains original theories of conscience amd moral judgment and it is the foundation for systemof morals.

Philosophy **ISBN:** *1-59462-777-0* **Pages:536**
MSRP $19.95

Jessica's First Prayer
Hesba Stretton

QTY

In a screened and secluded corner of one of the many railway-bridges which span the streets of London there could be seen a few years ago, from five o'clock every morning until half past eight, a tidily set-out coffee-stall, consisting of a trestle and board, upon which stood two large tin cans, with a small fire of charcoal burning under each so as to keep the coffee boiling during the early hours of the morning when the work-people were thronging into the city on their way to their daily toil...

Childrens **ISBN:** *1-59462-373-2* **Pages:84**
MSRP $9.95

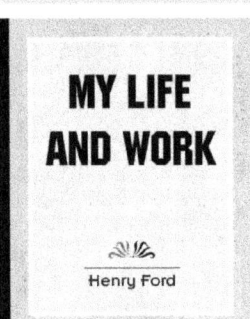

My Life and Work
Henry Ford

QTY

Henry Ford revolutionized the world with his implementation of mass production for the Model T automobile. Gain valuable business insight into his life and work with his own auto-biography... "We have only started on our development of our country we have not as yet, with all our talk of wonderful progress, done more than scratch the surface. The progress has been wonderful enough but..."

Biographies/ **ISBN:** *1-59462-198-5* **Pages:300**
MSRP $21.95

www.bookjungle.com *email: sales@bookjungle.com fax: 630-214-0564 mail: Book Jungle PO Box 2226 Champaign, IL 61825*

The Art of Cross-Examination
Francis Wellman

QTY

I presume it is the experience of every author, after his first book is published upon an important subject, to be almost overwhelmed with a wealth of ideas and illustrations which could readily have been included in his book, and which to his own mind, at least, seem to make a second edition inevitable. Such certainly was the case with me; and when the first edition had reached its sixth impression in five months, I rejoiced to learn that it seemed to my publishers that the book had met with a sufficiently favorable reception to justify a second and considerably enlarged edition. ..

Reference   ISBN: *1-59462-647-2*   Pages:412   MSRP *$19.95*

On the Duty of Civil Disobedience
Henry David Thoreau

QTY

Thoreau wrote his famous essay, On the Duty of Civil Disobedience, as a protest against an unjust but popular war and the immoral but popular institution of slave-owning. He did more than write—he declined to pay his taxes, and was hauled off to gaol in consequence. Who can say how much this refusal of his hastened the end of the war and of slavery ?

Law   ISBN: *1-59462-747-9*   Pages:48   MSRP *$7.45*

Dream Psychology Psychoanalysis for Beginners
Sigmund Freud

QTY

Sigmund Freud, born Sigismund Schlomo Freud (May 6, 1856 - September 23, 1939), was a Jewish-Austrian neurologist and psychiatrist who co-founded the psychoanalytic school of psychology. Freud is best known for his theories of the unconscious mind, especially involving the mechanism of repression; his redefinition of sexual desire as mobile and directed towards a wide variety of objects; and his therapeutic techniques, especially his understanding of transference in the therapeutic relationship and the presumed value of dreams as sources of insight into unconscious desires.

Psychology   ISBN: *1-59462-905-6*   Pages:196   MSRP *$15.45*

The Miracle of Right Thought
Orison Swett Marden

QTY

Believe with all of your heart that you will do what you were made to do. When the mind has once formed the habit of holding cheerful, happy, prosperous pictures, it will not be easy to form the opposite habit. It does not matter how improbable or how far away this realization may see, or how dark the prospects may be, if we visualize them as best we can, as vividly as possible, hold tenaciously to them and vigorously struggle to attain them, they will gradually become actualized, realized in the life. But a desire, a longing without endeavor, a yearning abandoned or held indifferently will vanish without realization.

Self Help   ISBN: *1-59462-644-8*   Pages:360   MSRP *$25.45*

www.bookjungle.com *email: sales@bookjungle.com fax: 630-214-0564 mail: Book Jungle PO Box 2226 Champaign, IL 61825*

QTY

	Title	ISBN	Price
☐	**The Rosicrucian Cosmo-Conception Mystic Christianity** by **Max Heindel**	ISBN: *1-59462-188-8*	**$38.95**

The Rosicrucian Cosmo-conception is not dogmatic, neither does it appeal to any other authority than the reason of the student. It is: not controversial, but is: sent forth in the, hope that it may help to clear... — *New Age/Religion Pages 646*

☐ **Abandonment To Divine Providence** by *Jean-Pierre de Caussade* — ISBN: *1-59462-228-0* **$25.95**
"The Rev. Jean Pierre de Caussade was one of the most remarkable spiritual writers of the Society of Jesus in France in the 18th Century. His death took place at Toulouse in 1751. His works have gone through many editions and have been republished... — *Inspirational/Religion Pages 400*

☐ **Mental Chemistry** by **Charles Haanel** — ISBN: *1-59462-192-6* **$23.95**
Mental Chemistry allows the change of material conditions by combining and appropriately utilizing the power of the mind. Much like applied chemistry creates something new and unique out of careful combinations of chemicals the mastery of mental chemistry... — *New Age Pages 354*

☐ **The Letters of Robert Browning and Elizabeth Barret Barrett 1845-1846 vol II** by **Robert Browning** and **Elizabeth Barrett** — ISBN: *1-59462-193-4* **$35.95** — *Biographies Pages 596*

☐ **Gleanings In Genesis (volume I)** by **Arthur W. Pink** — ISBN: *1-59462-130-6* **$27.45**
Appropriately has Genesis been termed "the seed plot of the Bible" for in it we have, in germ form, almost all of the great doctrines which are afterwards fully developed in the books of Scripture which follow... — *Religion/Inspirational Pages 420*

☐ **The Master Key** by **L. W. de Laurence** — ISBN: *1-59462-001-6* **$30.95**
In no branch of human knowledge has there been a more lively increase of the spirit of research during the past few years than in the study of Psychology, Concentration and Mental Discipline. The requests for authentic lessons in Thought Control, Mental Discipline and... — *New Age/Business Pages 422*

☐ **The Lesser Key Of Solomon Goetia** by **L. W. de Laurence** — ISBN: *1-59462-092-X* **$9.95**
This translation of the first book of the "Lernegton" which is now for the first time made accessible to students of Talismanic Magic was done, after careful collation and edition, from numerous Ancient Manuscripts in Hebrew, Latin, and French... — *New Age/Occult Pages 92*

☐ **Rubaiyat Of Omar Khayyam** by **Edward Fitzgerald** — ISBN:*1-59462-332-5* **$13.95**
Edward Fitzgerald, whom the world has already learned, in spite of his own efforts to remain within the shadow of anonymity, to look upon as one of the rarest poets of the century, was born at Bredfield, in Suffolk, on the 31st of March, 1809. He was the third son of John Purcell... — *Music Pages 172*

☐ **Ancient Law** by **Henry Maine** — ISBN: *1-59462-128-4* **$29.95**
The chief object of the following pages is to indicate some of the earliest ideas of mankind, as they are reflected in Ancient Law, and to point out the relation of those ideas to modern thought. — *Religiom/History Pages 452*

☐ **Far-Away Stories** by **William J. Locke** — ISBN: *1-59462-129-2* **$19.45**
"Good wine needs no bush, but a collection of mixed vintages does. And this book is just such a collection. Some of the stories I do not want to remain buried for ever in the museum files of dead magazine-numbers an author's not unpardonable vanity..." — *Fiction Pages 272*

☐ **Life of David Crockett** by **David Crockett** — ISBN: *1-59462-250-7* **$27.45**
"Colonel David Crockett was one of the most remarkable men of the times in which he lived. Born in humble life, but gifted with a strong will, an indomitable courage, and unremitting perseverance... — *Biographies/New Age Pages 424*

☐ **Lip-Reading** by **Edward Nitchie** — ISBN: *1-59462-206-X* **$25.95**
Edward B. Nitchie, founder of the New York School for the Hard of Hearing, now the Nitchie School of Lip-Reading, Inc, wrote "LIP-READING Principles and Practice". The development and perfecting of this meritorious work on lip-reading was an undertaking... — *How-to Pages 400*

☐ **A Handbook of Suggestive Therapeutics, Applied Hypnotism, Psychic Science** by **Henry Munro** — ISBN: *1-59462-214-0* **$24.95** — *Health/New Age/Health/Self-help Pages 376*

☐ **A Doll's House: and Two Other Plays** by **Henrik Ibsen** — ISBN: *1-59462-112-8* **$19.95**
Henrik Ibsen created this classic when in revolutionary 1848 Rome. Introducing some striking concepts in playwriting for the realist genre, this play has been studied the world over. — *Fiction/Classics/Plays 308*

☐ **The Light of Asia** by **sir Edwin Arnold** — ISBN: *1-59462-204-3* **$13.95**
In this poetic masterpiece, Edwin Arnold describes the life and teachings of Buddha. The man who was to become known as Buddha to the world was born as Prince Gautama of India but he rejected the worldly riches and abandoned the reigns of power when... — *Religion/History/Biographies Pages 170*

☐ **The Complete Works of Guy de Maupassant** by **Guy de Maupassant** — ISBN: *1-59462-157-8* **$16.95**
"For days and days, nights and nights, I had dreamed of that first kiss which was to consecrate our engagement, and I knew not on what spot I should put my lips..." — *Fiction/Classics Pages 240*

☐ **The Art of Cross-Examination** by **Francis L. Wellman** — ISBN: *1-59462-309-0* **$26.95**
Written by a renowned trial lawyer, Wellman imparts his experience and uses case studies to explain how to use psychology to extract desired information through questioning. — *How-to/Science/Reference Pages 408*

☐ **Answered or Unanswered?** by **Louisa Vaughan** — ISBN: *1-59462-248-5* **$10.95**
Miracles of Faith in China — *Religion Pages 112*

☐ **The Edinburgh Lectures on Mental Science (1909)** by **Thomas** — ISBN: *1-59462-008-3* **$11.95**
This book contains the substance of a course of lectures recently given by the writer in the Queen Street Hail, Edinburgh. Its purpose is to indicate the Natural Principles governing the relation between Mental Action and Material Conditions... — *New Age/Psychology Pages 148*

☐ **Ayesha** by **H. Rider Haggard** — ISBN: *1-59462-301-5* **$24.95**
Verily and indeed it is the unexpected that happens! Probably if there was one person upon the earth from whom the Editor of this, and of a certain previous history, did not expect to hear again... — *Classics Pages 380*

☐ **Ayala's Angel** by **Anthony Trollope** — ISBN: *1-59462-352-X* **$29.95**
The two girls were both pretty, but Lucy who was twenty-one who supposed to be simple and comparatively unattractive, whereas Ayala was credited, as her Bombwhat romantic name might show, with poetic charm and a taste for romance. Ayala when her father died was nineteen... — *Fiction Pages 484*

☐ **The American Commonwealth** by **James Bryce** — ISBN: *1-59462-286-8* **$34.45**
An interpretation of American democratic political theory. It examines political mechanics and society from the perspective of Scotsman James Bryce — *Politics Pages 572*

☐ **Stories of the Pilgrims** by **Margaret P. Pumphrey** — ISBN: *1-59462-116-0* **$17.95**
This book explores pilgrims religious oppression in England as well as their escape to Holland and eventual crossing to America on the Mayflower, and their early days in New England... — *History Pages 268*

www.bookjungle.com email: sales@bookjungle.com fax: 630-214-0564 mail: Book Jungle PO Box 2226 Champaign, IL 61825

		QTY
The Fasting Cure *by Sinclair Upton*	ISBN: *1-59462-222-1* **$13.95**	☐
In the Cosmopolitan Magazine for May, 1910, and in the Contemporary Review (London) for April, 1910, I published an article dealing with my experiences in fasting. I have written a great many magazine articles, but never one which attracted so much attention... New Age/Self Help/Health Pages 164		
Hebrew Astrology *by Sepharial*	ISBN: *1-59462-308-2* **$13.45**	☐
In these days of advanced thinking it is a matter of common observation that we have left many of the old landmarks behind and that we are now pressing forward to greater heights and to a wider horizon than that which represented the mind-content of our progenitors... Astrology Pages 144		
Thought Vibration or The Law of Attraction in the Thought World	ISBN: *1-59462-127-6* **$12.95**	☐
by William Walker Atkinson	Psychology/Religion Pages 144	
Optimism *by Helen Keller*	ISBN: *1-59462-108-X* **$15.95**	☐
Helen Keller was blind, deaf, and mute since 19 months old, yet famously learned how to overcome these handicaps, communicate with the world, and spread her lectures promoting optimism. An inspiring read for everyone... Biographies/Inspirational Pages 84		
Sara Crewe *by Frances Burnett*	ISBN: *1-59462-360-0* **$9.45**	☐
In the first place, Miss Minchin lived in London. Her home was a large, dull, tall one, in a large, dull square, where all the houses were alike, and all the sparrows were alike, and where all the door-knockers made the same heavy sound... Childrens/Classic Pages 88		
The Autobiography of Benjamin Franklin *by Benjamin Franklin*	ISBN: *1-59462-135-7* **$24.95**	☐
The Autobiography of Benjamin Franklin has probably been more extensively read than any other American historical work, and no other book of its kind has had such ups and downs of fortune. Franklin lived for many years in England, where he was agent... Biographies/History Pages 332		

Name	
Email	
Telephone	
Address	
City, State ZIP	

☐ Credit Card   ☐ Check / Money Order

Credit Card Number	
Expiration Date	
Signature	

Please Mail to: Book Jungle
                 PO Box 2226
                 Champaign, IL 61825
or Fax to: 630-214-0564

ORDERING INFORMATION

web: *www.bookjungle.com*
email: *sales@bookjungle.com*
fax: *630-214-0564*
mail: *Book Jungle PO Box 2226 Champaign, IL 61825*
or PayPal *to sales@bookjungle.com*

Please contact us for bulk discounts

DIRECT-ORDER TERMS

**20% Discount if You Order
Two or More Books**
Free Domestic Shipping!
Accepted: Master Card, Visa,
Discover, American Express

www.ingramcontent.com/pod-product-compliance
Lightning Source LLC
Chambersburg PA
CBHW081231170426
43198CB00017B/2718